THE KEY TO YOUR CHILD'S HEART

THE KEY TO YOUR CHILD'S HEART

♥ ♥ ♥ ♥ ♥ ♥ ♥ ♥ ♥ ♥ ♥ ♥ ♥ ♥ ♥ ♥ ♥

GARY SMALLEY

(with help from Kari, Gregory and Michael Smalley)

CARMEL • NEW YORK 10512

This Guideposts edition is published by
special arrangement with Word, Inc.

THE KEY TO YOUR CHILD'S HEART

Library of Congress Cataloging in Publication Data

Smalley, Gary.
The key to your child's heart.

  Bibliography: p.
  1. Parenting—Religious aspects—Christianity.
2. Child rearing—Religious aspects—Christianity.
I. Title.
BV4529.S47   1984   649'.1   84-15288
ISBN 0-8499-0433-1

Printed in the United States of America

In loving memory of our parents,
Uel Jefferson and Eleanor Deck
Frank and Emily Smalley.
And to our children,
Kari, Greg and Michael,
we present to you our lifetime commitment.

Contents

7

Contents

It is with special appreciation that I acknowledge my debt to those without whose help this book could never have been published. To Judy Pitzmier for her dedication, talent, and warm understanding during the many hours of editing. To Al Janssen for his tremendous inspiration, encouragement, and editing skills when I couldn't "see the end." To Bill Yarger and B. John Trent, two of my outstanding and supportive pastors, who carefully evaluated the final draft. Last but certainly not least, to my wife, Norma, who walked with me every step of the way writing this book.

The Key to Your Child's Heart

We were enduring our twelfth consecutive day of rain while traveling across country one summer. Everything in our mini-motorhome was damp, and all five of us were tired of each other.

We had taken a drive up into Canada to see the beauty of Banff National Park. I had described the beautiful mountains and rivers we would see, but for three straight days, fog and rain had concealed the scenic beauty. Now on the fourth morning, we were sitting in a restaurant trying to decide what to do. I urged us to return to our home in Phoenix where it was warm and dry. I'd fly alone from there to my next speaking engagement in Seattle. My wife, Norma, pleaded that we stay a fourth day in Canada and wait for the sun to break through. Kari, our fifteen-year-old daughter, wanted us to continue driving to Seattle. Our two younger boys "demanded" fishing in Washington.

As our volume increased in defense of each plan, Greg, our middle child, shouted, "Stop! I've got the solution!" He was so emphatic that even our neighbors in the next booth stopped to listen. "I think we ought to go out in the camper, get the gun and shoot each other." All of us burst out laughing and that relaxed us enough to stay put another day during which the sun finally revealed the majesty of the Canadian Rockies.

Why is it that all five of us, and other families similar to ours, can go through very strained times like what we experienced in Canada and still witness a closeness and happiness together? Yet there are many other families that are so divided that even a minor crisis can permanently scatter the members in different directions.

There are many outstanding books on raising children, yet after reading some, I have often wondered "What's the use in trying? It's too difficult!" In my speaking and counseling all across the nation, I have found that many parents experience similar frustration and guilt.

In this book, you'll discover that we're an average family with very typical conflicts. But we have tried to find solutions to those conflicts that can be applied to almost every family. We will recount what has and has not worked in our home and will share with you the main factors that have drawn us into close relationship.

We'll also be summarizing what some of the parenting experts are saying today. For example, there are four basic types of parents. But only one of those four types produces the best results in children. We will examine why the children of these parents have much greater self-worth, are less rebellious, and are generally more successful in life.

You'll read about how we brought order and harmony to our family through the simple method of "contracts."
We will discuss several practical ways to help protect a

child from becoming sexually involved before marriage.

If you're wondering how to get your children to clean their rooms, eat healthier foods, and avoid certain harmful activities, we have at least twenty-two ways to motivate your children. We will even share the secret of how you can actually increase your children's desire to listen carefully to you.

This book will give you several basic principles that I believe are *key* to raising children. In particular, the next chapter covers one principle that if diligently applied can virtually guarantee a closer relationship between parent and child. In my opinion, it is *The Key to Your Child's Heart*.

Violation of this principle has undoubtedly destroyed more families than any other single factor. It is the major reason why over one million children have run away from home and why millions more reject their parents' moral values and standards. Fewer teenagers would misuse alcohol and drugs if parents understood and practiced this principle.

Therefore, the concept presented in the next chapter provides the foundation for successful parenting. I suggest that you may want to reread it several times. Master this principle and I can assure that you will make significant progress towards experiencing the joys and rewards of a closer-knit family.

1

How to Overcome the Major Destroyer of Families

- *A Closed Spirit*
- *Manifestations of a Closed Spirit*
- *Reopening a Child's Spirit*
- *Five Steps to Reopen a Child's Spirit*
- *Reasons Why One Might Refuse to Forgive*
- *Observing Voice Tone and Facial Expressions to Recognize a Closed Spirit*
- *How a Child or an Adult Can Reopen His Own Spirit*
- *How Open Is Your Child's Spirit?*
- *84 Ways We Can Offend Our Children*

One evening, while I was in my bedroom on a long-distance phone call, my son Greg, five years old at the time, let out a bloodcurdling scream from the master bathroom. He came running to the door, screaming so loudly that I couldn't hear the other person's voice. I could feel my blood pressure rise as I signaled for him to be quiet. I dramatically patted my bottom to let him know what was coming if he didn't shut up immediately. But Greg continued to scream, so I quickly ended my phone conversation, telling the person I'd get back to him later.

When I hung up the phone, I grabbed Greg by the arm and shook him. "Why are you screaming?" I demanded. "Couldn't you see I was on the phone?"

Without waiting for an answer, I shoved him into the hall and said, "You get into your bedroom right now." He fell when I pushed him, but got back up, still crying, and hurried into his room. I grabbed the paddle we used for spanking—the entire family had helped decorate it—and told him to lie down on his bed. Then I gave him several hard swats. Satisfied with my discipline, I stood back and thought, *That's what you get for violating my rule.* You see, no one was supposed to scream while I was on the phone—I wouldn't want people to think my family was out of control.

It was our custom after a spanking to hold the child and reaffirm our love for him. But this time, something took place that scared me. Greg was still crying. He stood up and the look in his eyes said, "I hate you." He backed away from me to let me know that he didn't want me to touch him. I suddenly realized what I had done, and I knew that if I didn't take immediate action, there might be serious consequences in our relationship. Fortunately, someone had taught me what to do, and within a few moments, we were hugging each other on his bed, back in full fellowship and harmony.

What actually took place has saved our family time and time again from drifting into deep conflict. The principle I am about to share has, without a doubt, been the single most significant factor in establishing and maintaining harmony in our home.

In the United States, we are suffering from an overwhelming epidemic of broken relationships. We don't have to look hard to see the evidence. We see it to some degree in every relationship, both inside and outside of the home. I hope that I can explain in these next few pages what I know can have a very positive effect on all relationships, especially with our children.

I have taken what I've observed during my more than twenty years counseling, with my own family, and what I've learned from experts in the field of building personal relationships. I've tried to develop a simple system of explaining the major factor that causes disharmony within the home, as well as outside of it. I would urge you again to reread this one chapter many times because I have found it to be *the key* to staying in harmony with *anyone*.

A Closed Spirit

The single most prevalent cause of disharmony within a home is what I have labeled *a closed spirit.*

What do I mean by a closed spirit? What causes it? Let's begin by saying that every person is born with a spirit, soul, and body, and all three are interrelated. I will define spirit as a person's innermost being, similar to his conscience. It's the area in which people can have fellowship with one another and enjoy each other's presence without a word being spoken. Our deepest relationships are built on the spirit level. The *soul* would include our mind, will, and emotions. The *body* is, of course, our physical makeup. Together, we'll say the three comprise a total person.

The soul and the body are within the spirit, something like the diagram on the next page.

To help us understand how the spirit, soul, and body operate together, let's look at an example from nature. When I was a child, I enjoyed observing sea urchins on the California coast. They were often found in tidal pools among the rocks. About four or five inches in diameter, they look like colorful flowers with soft, wavy tentacles. But I noticed an interesting phenomenon. Sometimes I'd take a stick and poke one of them. Immediately the sea urchin would withdraw its sensitive tentacles and close up until it became a shell. It was similar to a beautiful flower closing. Now it was protected from further injury.

What happens with the sea urchin illustrates what happens to a person when he is offended. The tentacles of that sea urchin are similar to the spirit of a person. The

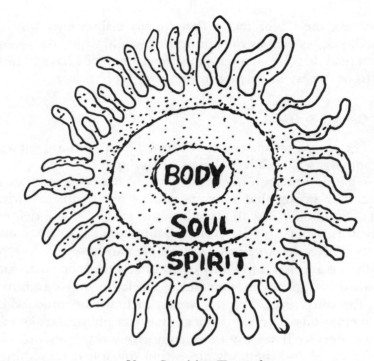

Very Sensitive Tentacles

sea urchin is completely open and vulnerable. But when the stick pokes him, he closes up. In a similar way, when a person is offended, he closes up. When his spirit closes, it in turn closes his soul and body. If the spirit is open, so are the soul and body. In other words, when the spirits of two people are open, they enjoy talking (soul) and touching (body). If the spirit closes, the soul and body close to the same degree. A person with a closed spirit will usually avoid communication.

This is what I saw happening to Greg. When I pushed him in the hallway and screamed at him in harshness, *I had poked his spirit.* The greater the harshness, the greater the pain a person feels in his spirit. My harshness, pushing,

Closing Tentacles

and spanking without finding out the facts were three large poking sticks. Like the sea urchin, Greg closed his spirit to me with each jab. And when he closed his spirit, he closed everything else. He didn't like me. He didn't want to be near me. He didn't want to talk to me. And he resisted my attempts to touch him. These were the keys that told me that his spirit was closing. When a child resists affection—if you touch his hand and it's cold and limp, or if you put your arm around her and she turns her back, shrugs you off, and avoids conversation—that usually means the spirit is closing.

Manifestations of a Closed Spirit

When a child's spirit is closing there are many possible manifestations. He may argue and resist when you ask him to do something. He may be contrary, refusing to like anything you like! He may withdraw, and usually he is not very responsive to affection.

If his spirit is closed further, he may seek friends who are opposite from the kinds of friends you want him to

21

have. He may swear or use disrespectful language. A closed spirit is a major cause for the misuse of drugs and alcohol, and a primary reason why children become sexually permissive.

At the very worst, a child whose spirit has been completely closed may run away from home or commit suicide.

All of these are symptoms of a closed spirit. If we can recognize it, and help to reopen the spirit, we will often take care of the symptoms in the process.

During my years of counseling, I've come to realize that this principle is the key to most relationships. When a man can't stand his boss, it's primarily because his spirit was "stepped on" or "poked." So the employee usually avoids his boss, silently disagreeing and resisting him. I see it all the time with professional athletes. They get offended by management or coaches and suddenly announce they want to be traded. Where once they were thrilled to be on the team, now they want to get away from it.

It happens in dating. When a girl meets a guy, usually her spirit is wide open to him. She likes him. She wants to talk with him. She enjoys doing things with him. When he touches her, she responds positively. Then something happens and suddenly she isn't as open. She guards her emotions more carefully and isn't as free with her affection. Somehow, her boyfriend has been closing her spirit, often without even knowing it.

It happens all the time in marriage. For years I did many little things to close Norma's spirit. I enjoyed telling little jokes about her to my friends or to my audiences when I spoke. I'd say things like "My wife treats me like a God. Every morning she serves me burnt offerings." Or this one: "Being married to Norma is like being married to an angel. Every day she's up in the air, harping about something, and she never has an earthly thing to wear." I'd laugh and others would laugh, but Norma wouldn't laugh. When she tried to express her hurt, I'd answer, "Come on! Can't you take a joke?"

What I didn't realize is that my jokes, kidding, sarcastic comments, and insensitive actions were closing her spirit a little more each time. After several years of marriage, Norma had closed much of her spirit to me. But I didn't know it. I only saw the outward results like the times when I'd come home from work and she wouldn't greet me. I'd say, "Hi, Hon, I'm home," and there'd be no response. I'd ask, "Is there anything wrong," and she'd say, "No." Gradually I began to learn that "No" really meant "Yes." I needed to find out how I had closed her spirit, and take the steps necessary to reopen it.

During my seminars, to demonstrate how sensitive the spirit is, I often ask a man to come forward, close his eyes, and hold out his hand. First I put a large rock in his hand and ask him to identify the object. He usually correctly identifies it as a rock. Then I replace the rock with a pebble. Usually he can't identify it without feeling it for awhile. Most men, when they say something offensive to their wives, think they are only dropping a small pebble on her spirit. But she feels it like a large rock, which can close her spirit.

The same thing can happen in all relationships, especially between parents and their children. This is particularly dangerous with young children who need a lot of physical affection—touching and hugging. If a parent is harsh with a daughter, so that she is offended, she will begin closing her spirit. But she still needs to be touched, and since she won't accept touching from Mom or Dad, she looks elsewhere.

Young men can easily pick up her need for affection and take advantage of her. She may resist at first, not wanting to compromise her standards, but her resistance breaks down with the boy's persistence. Because she has already closed her spirit to her parents and she can't take any more rejection, she has a tendency to give in to the boy. If, on the other hand, her relationship with Mom and Dad is solid, her spirit open, and there has been a healthy degree of affection and touching between them, she is much more likely to have the energy and desire to maintain her moral standards.

Boys have a similar need for affection. However, some fathers won't hug their sons because they think it's not manly. And some have caused their son's spirit to be closed so that their sons reject any affection. It has been determined that this lack of affection may cause boys to find affection in ways that can even lead to a homosexual relationship. Dr. Ross Campbell, a psychiatrist who specializes in working with children, has discovered that in all his reading and experience, he has never known of one sexually disoriented person who had a warm, loving, and *affectionate* father.

If, on the other hand, a parent is cold and offensive, a son can close his spirit, and many times adopt rebellious, antisocial behavior.

Fortunately, a child's spirit is somewhat pliable for the first several years. When children are offended, they are willing and ready to get back into harmony. But if we don't recognize when a child's spirit is closing, we can reap disastrous results.

A closed spirit can also occur between children. Once, Michael, our youngest child, exploded in anger at Greg to the point where he was ready to start slugging it out. When I intervened, I learned that Greg had been harsh with Mike, but Mike was responding far more vehemently than was normal. So I knew something else was wrong.

Alone with Michael, I started playing "twenty questions" trying to discover what had caused his spirit to close. I asked, "Did your sister hurt you?" "Was it me?" "Mom?"

Finally, when I asked him if anything had happened to him at school, he put his head down and continued crying. Up to this point, Michael refused to tell me anything. Many times children will say they do not want to talk, but they really do. They will often open up when we *gently* probe to discover their problem.

Michael went on to tell me that his best friend at school had chosen a new friend, and the two of them had turned against him. My heart went out to him as he cried and I wanted to hold him, but he wasn't ready yet. That told me there was still another problem. Then Michael revealed that Greg and his friend across the street wouldn't play with him. The neighbor was taking his brother away from him. It was just like what had happened at school.

I told him that I felt terrible and asked if I could hold him. He scooted across the bed and held me, crying and feeling the full pain of rejection. Later on we got together with Greg, and Michael explained to him how he felt about the neighbor across the street. Together, the three of us were able to resolve the problem by taking the necessary steps to open Mike's spirit.

If I had not learned that Michael's spirit was closing toward Greg and his friend at school, I might have compounded the problem. I could have said, "Michael, shape up. You're getting to be a big boy now. I'm tired of the way you fight with Greg." That would have closed his spirit even more, especially toward me. Being harsh and demanding is like a big stick "poking" a person's spirit and causing it to close.

In the average home, it is impossible to keep from offending each other. Something seems to happen almost every day that will cause someone to be offended. *Yet, it is possible to stay in harmony as long as we resolve each offense.* One offense on top of another, on top of another, can build a wall cementing the spirit shut. It is much easier to reopen a child's spirit when it is closed slightly through one or only a few small offenses. But it is still possible to reopen a child's spirit even in the worst situations.

Reopening a Child's Spirit

There are undoubtedly many ways to help open a person's spirit that has closed toward us. I'll mention five ways that have been the most effective in our family and in my counseling. I'll show them in a particular order because this is how I've observed them to be most helpful. However, you may find it more effective to rearrange them or add other ways to the list.

Each of the five steps were used after I had spanked Greg for screaming while I was on the phone. After applying them, I witnessed his spirit reopen in a matter of minutes. Here is the sequence:

Once I had realized that Greg's spirit was closing toward me, I dropped to my knees and my attitude became *soft and tender.* Gently, I asked him, "Greg, *why* were you screaming in the bathroom?" with his voice trembling as he fought back the tears, he managed to say, "I fell and hit my ear on the bathtub." He showed me his ear which was swollen and bleeding. When I saw what had happened, I felt terrible. I gently said to him, "Greg, *I was so wrong* to have treated you this way. Daddy's the one who deserved the spanking." Greg wiped his tears and added, "Then when you pushed me in the hall, I hit my same ear on the toy box."

By this time, I felt like a child abuser. I was an irresponsible father and I recognized it. "Greg, Daddy was wrong." I handed him the spanking stick. "I'm the one who deserves to be spanked. I'm the one who needs it." He grabbed the stick and dropped it. He backed up again, still not wanting any part of me. I wanted to reach out and touch him, but his spirit was still closed toward me.

Finally, I said, again tenderly, "Greg, I was wrong. I know I don't deserve it, but I wonder if it would be possible for you to find it in your heart to *forgive me.*" Immediately he threw his arms around me. We fell back against the bed and he laid on my chest for about a half hour as we held each other tightly. After some time, I looked at his ear again and asked, "Are you sure we're o.k. now?" "Yes, Daddy, I forgive you," he said, patting me on the back, "We all make mistakes." From the tone of his voice and the way he touched me, I knew his spirit was opening again.

It may take a little more time for some children to reopen their spirits, depending on the circumstances; but a child is certainly worth our time.

Let's go back now and examine more carefully each of the five ways to open a person's closed spirit.

Five Steps to Reopen a Child's Spirit

1. Become Tender-Hearted

The first step that I needed to take to open Greg's spirit was *to reflect tenderness and softness.* Gentleness has a way of melting anger.

As we attempt to open one's spirit, our body language, our muscles, our facial expressions, and our tone of voice, must become soft, gentle, tender, and caring. By doing this, we are communicating several things to the person whom we have offended:

We're saying:

(a) He is valuable and important. We express this importance in nonverbal ways. We are slow to move toward

27

him. Our heads may be bowed down, and we are obviously grieved that we have hurt him.

(b) We do not want to see his spirit closed; we care about him.

(c) We know there is something wrong. We acknowledge by our softness that an offense has taken place and we are going to *slow down* long enough to correct whatever has happened.

(d) We are open to listen. It is safe for him to share what has happened and we are not going to get angry or hurt him again.

I was counseling a pro football player and his wife, and she was sharing with me how deeply offended she had been by some of the things her husband had said and done. He said he didn't understand why she got so mad and upset about the things he was doing. I could see she was hurting and that her spirit was closing toward him. So I asked him if he wanted to work on opening her spirit. He agreed to try.

"I want you to become really tender right now and put your arm around your wife," I said. "Pretend that your whole body is melting ice cream. Gently tell her that you know you have hurt her and you want to resolve it."

He started to do as I said, putting his arm around her, and she said, "Oh, you don't mean that!" Rather than understanding how hurt she was, he reacted: "I do too mean that. Don't tell me I don't mean this." The athlete was listening to his wife's words, rather than to the tone of her voice which was telling him how closed her spirit was. His anger and harshness was only further closing her spirit.

I suggested he let me demonstrate what I meant. Immediately, my voice softened and I became caring and gentle. I reached across the table and touched her hand and said, "You're really hurting, aren't you? And I know that the things I have done to you have deeply affected you." With my softness her facial muscles began to relax. Her head slightly bowed, her eyes started to fill with tears. Both of us were amazed how quickly her spirit was willing to open.

I find that the same thing happens with our children. Tenderness melts the anger and it begins to open their spirits.

2. Increase Understanding

The second step to open the spirit of a person is to *increase our understanding of the pain he feels and how he has interpreted our offensive behavior.* When I asked Greg why he was crying and he said it was because he had fallen against the bathtub, my understanding of his pain immediately increased. I already was soft but my spirit became even softer because I had deeper understanding and could feel his hurt feelings. I probably would have screamed, too, no matter what the rule was, if I had fallen against the bathtub. Many times just these two factors—being *soft* and then *understanding* a person's pain—will open a person's spirit.

Children in various household arrangements often dream that someday someone will understand what they are feeling and how they are hurting. Where there are single parents or blended families through a second marriage, a child can feel deeply offended by the partner who leaves or by new members of a family he's thrust into. Oftentimes a child will blame himself for a divorce. He may not say anything to either one of the parents, but he begins to express the symptoms of a closed spirit. He is argumentative and avoids his parents, even to the point of not allowing them to touch him. Either parent can begin to solve this problem by softening his heart toward that child and gaining more understanding of his pain.

One of the best ways to increase understanding of a child's hurt is through emotional word pictures. They help us feel the child's pain in such a vivid way that some conflicts are resolved in seconds.

One boy, whose father constantly criticized him, told his dad, "I sometimes feel like a bird in a nest. You fly in, and I should feel so encouraged to see you, because you are going to have some food or encouragement for me, but instead you jerk off one of the branches or little fibers that holds the nest together and fly away. I begin to think, 'Wait a minute. He's tearing this nest apart and I'm not ready to fly yet.' I have such an insecure feeling when I see you coming because you're always picking on me, tearing me down, and it's just like pulling those little pieces of string out of that nest." When the boy's father heard this word picture, he felt his son's hurt and insecurity. This one emotional word picture helped this father greatly reduce his criticism of his son.

As parents, we can ask our children to help us understand their feelings by asking them questions like, "If you were a rabbit, what would be happening to you right now because of what I just did?" or, "If you were a piece of cloth what would you look like?" or, "Give me a color to describe how you are feeling." Usually, if we give them time and encouragement, children can tell us exactly how they feel. If my daughter tells me she is feeling really blue, I might ask if it is a dark blue or a light blue, and if there are any cheerful spots in the color. One boy whose father traveled extensively said, "Dad, the way you've been avoiding me lately, I feel like a dishrag under the sink that's had a steady drip on it for the last two months. Nobody has noticed it so now it's rotten and mildewey." Most any parent could feel the pain of mildew.

We can also help our children express their feelings by relating to previous experiences. We can help them by saying, "Remember the time your friend across the street rejected you and wouldn't play with you? Am I sort of making you feel like that?" or, "Remember how you felt in school when you got that F, when you really studied hard for an A? Then your classmates made fun of you, and remember how you were embarrassed? Is that sort of how you felt today when I corrected you in front of your friends?"

Emotional word pictures are such an important tool in communication that we will talk more about using them in another chapter. It is very important that children know we really understand how they feel when they are offended. If a child refuses to talk, it may take a "cooling off" period for both child and parent. After a few minutes, a parent can continue gently probing to discover the level of hurt. Give a child time to understand his own emotional pain.

3. Recognize the Offense

The third step in opening a person's spirit is *admitting that we were wrong*, because what we did was offensive to him. It could even be that what we did was not wrong, but *how* we did it—our attitude was wrong. For example, I could spank my child for the right reason, but if I spank him in harsh anger, I need to admit my wrong attitude.

Even the world recognizes the importance of confession and admission of guilt. When Soviet fighter planes shot down a Korean 747 killing the more than 250 passengers, the world was shocked. Immediately, a number of the free-world countries demanded that Russia admit they were wrong and apologize. News commentators emphasized a previous example when Israel shot down a Libyan passenger airliner, and how they apologized to the world and paid restitution to all the passengers' families. But when the Soviets failed to admit they were wrong, and failed to make restitution, the free-world became even angrier and more hardened toward them.

Children tend to be more aware of their own needs and wants and less concerned about the welfare of others. This self-awareness or self-centeredness increases the possibility of their being offended. As they grow in maturity, they find that people don't offend them as much, because they have become more understanding of people.

As parents, we must be wise enough to know what our child's level of maturity is so that we don't close his spirit unnecessarily. If we offend our child because he is immature, we can say, "I was wrong to treat you this way." We don't add, "You are only hurt because you are so immature." That would only offend them all the more.

One of the hardest things for many parents to do is to admit when they are wrong. It's especially hard for fathers. I do not necessarily like to find out when I am wrong and it's not always easy to admit when I am. But I must remember that a hardened, resistant attitude is extremely detrimental to children.

As a child hears his parents admit it when they are offensive and sees that they understand how he feels, he gains a feeling of importance. He realizes that he is a valuable person. Sometimes this is all it takes to open a child's spirit. But we should be careful because there are two more factors that are important to make sure that the spirit has reopened.

4. Attempt to Touch

The fourth factor is *attempting to touch the offended person.* There are several reasons why we want to touch a child when he has been offended. First of all, he needs to be touched. If he reaches out and responds to our touching, then we know his spirit is opening or has completely reopened. This is an extremely important time to take him tenderly in our arms and hold him for awhile. It lets him know that we care, that we love him, and that he is very important.

Second, touching allows us to find out if the child's spirit is not opening. Perhaps the offense was deeper than we realized. Or he may have been offended by someone outside the family, like Mike with his friend at school, and he has a general resentment toward everyone around him. If I have admitted I am wrong, am soft and understanding, and reach out to touch my child but he pulls back or moves away, it is an indication that he isn't ready to open his spirit. He may need more time or a greater understanding from the one who offended him.

When parents are not accustomed to touching their children, like my own parents who were reluctant to touch each other as well as their six kids, they may want to "warn" or explain to their children why they're starting to touch. A child who hasn't been touched may feel somewhat hesitant to allow touching even if his spirit is open. A gradual adjustment may be necessary.

Obviously, the lack of touching doesn't always mean that we have closed our child's spirit. Children go through stages where they may avoid touching, for example during puberty. However, if a parent is maintaining harmony with his child, he can usually detect if the child is offended or just passing through a stage.

There might be other reasons why our child resists our touch. One summer our family went fishing in the Colorado mountains. I offended Kari by being harsh. She had hurt her knee and I was trying to force her quickly up the bank so I could get back to my fishing. About halfway up the bank, I realized that I had hurt her spirit, and that she was far more important than my fishing. So I stopped, took her in my arms and told her I knew I had offended her and that I was wrong. She wiggled out of my grasp and asked, "Dad, did you use any deodorant today?"

5. Seek Forgiveness

The final step to open someone's spirit is to *seek forgiveness from the one offended.* When we have offended someone, we must give him a chance to respond. For me, the best

33

way is to say something like, "Could you find it in your heart to forgive me?" This is when I knew I had reopened Greg's spirit, for when I asked for his forgiveness, he rushed into my arms. We can say at this point that *true restoration is confession of wrong plus forgiveness granted.*

Reasons Why One Might Refuse to Forgive

If we have followed these five steps and the child refuses to forgive us, there are several possible reasons.

Perhaps the offense was deeper than we realized. Or he may have been offended by someone outside the family and so he has a general resentment toward everyone around him. Maybe we rushed things and the child didn't have time to think through what happened. He may think that a parent can't possibly understand how he has been hurt and simply asking forgiveness doesn't erase everything. Or perhaps the child might also want to see a real change in the parent's behavior first.

Whatever the reason, I have discovered that the best thing to do is start all over again. Be patient; don't rush. Begin at number one and continue to be soft and tender. Go to number two and increase our understanding. We can even say things like, "You know, I probably don't know how much you are hurting." Repeat that you are wrong. "I don't deserve to be forgiven for the way I have treated you lately, but I pray that you can. I want you to know that I love you and I was wrong. I really mean that." At this point, reach out and touch him on the arm to see if he has softened. If he hasn't, give him some time, but be persistent. And finally, ask for his forgiveness again.

One mistake many parents make is dropping the issue altogether. "Well, if he won't forgive me, that's his problem. I did my part." With that attitude, the problem may never be resolved. It's better to back off for awhile, allow a few minutes or even hours for things to cool down, then come back and repeat these five steps.

As parents, there is one additional effective way we can detect a closed spirit. I've found that if we carefully watch nonverbal expressions, we can add to our understanding of what's going on inside a child.

Observing Voice Tone and Facial Expressions to Recognize a Closed Spirit

One woman said to me after a seminar, "I hate my husband. I hate him so much that I can't even talk about him. I'll never go back to him." Yet four months later, that same woman was back with her husband and they were living together in harmony. I heard one husband say about his wife, "I hate that woman so much I can't even stand to look at her." Within hours that same man was loving his wife and regaining his feelings and desires for her.

Sometimes it takes several months, but I'm finding that regaining harmony *is* possible. My own hope for families and couples increases almost daily because I'm now aware that surface words like, "I hate you, I'll never live with you again, I'll always hate you," are reflections of a closed spirit.

A child may say to his parents, "I hate you. I can't handle any more of this. I'm through with this family. I've had it up to here and I don't want to talk about it. I don't even want to be around here." When people spew forth such words, I find they really are saying that they want to talk about it. They would love to resolve the problem but they want to resolve it in a certain way. We need to listen to how they say it, with what intensity. Learn to watch their facial expressions and listen to their tone of voice instead of limiting our understanding to the words they use.

Imagine for a moment a scale from zero to ten, with zero indicating the spirit is totally open and ten totally closed. If I reach for my daughter's hand after I have offended her and she turns her back to me and says, "Dad, you always do this to me and I just can't handle it anymore," chances are I have closed her spirit to about a three. It is not really major, yet it's still very important to reopen it. If I go to touch her and she jerks away from me and says, "Dad, just leave me alone. You're always doing this to me and I just feel like running away," her spirit is probably closed about halfway. But let's say that I knock on her bedroom door and she asks, "Who is it?" in a very hostile voice. I open the door and she says, "Just get out of here, Dad," and she takes a vase and throws it at me. I duck in time and say, "Hey, I know I was wrong . . ." but she yells, "I'm going to run away from this place. I just hate it around here." Those words and actions tell me that her spirit is closed to probably an eight or nine. Usually, the more violent and hostile the resistance, the tighter the spirit has been closed. Hostility may settle into apathy or indifference indicating "my spirit is cemented closed, don't try to reopen it." But when we realize that one's words don't necessarily reflect how one feels inside, we can continue to gently pry open someone's spirit.

The best way that I know to deal with such surface words is to become soft and understanding and admit we are wrong. Then persevere until we can touch and seek forgiveness. That is what they really want. But it may take time.

I have also found that offenses which happened many years ago can still be resolved in much the same way. A child may remember being hurt by a parent many years before. And if a parent really wants to make sure that a child's spirit is totally open toward him, it is appropriate to go back into the past and bring up these old offenses, *as long as the offenses are resolved once they are brought up.*

How a Child or an Adult Can Reopen His Own Spirit

If parents are not willing to open their child's closed spirit, it would sound as though the child was destined to rebellion. But there are several things that a child or anyone can do to open his own spirit.

This simple but profound truth is taught in a prayer prayed millions of times each year—the Lord's Prayer. I had read this prayer for years, but continued to miss its true meaning. The prayer invites us to forgive those who trespass against us—who offend us—then God will forgive us of our trespasses. But if we refuse to forgive those who trespass against us, then God will not forgive us.

The word forgive comes from a Greek word meaning "to release" or "set free." It means to untie the chains that bind people. Therefore, when we set free those who offend us or trespass against us, God unties us, opening our spirit. He cannot reopen our spirit, however, if we refuse to help those who have hurt us.

Corrie ten Boom, who helped many Jews escape the German torture camps in World War II, told me a story that illustrated what Jesus meant by His prayer. Sometime after she had been released from a concentration camp, she spoke at a church in Germany. As the crowd filed out after the service, she saw a man working his way forward. With horror, she recognized him. He had been a guard—one of the most cruel—in the concentration camp where she and her sister had been interned. He had actually been instrumental in causing the death of her sister, Betsie. She was almost nauseated by him. Her spirit had already been closed toward him years before. He reached out his hand and said, "Corrie ten Boom, I have become a Christian and I know God has forgiven me for the cruel things I did. But I've come to ask if you would forgive me." Corrie said her arms were frozen to her side. She couldn't move.

She told me it was the most difficult thing she'd ever done, but she did reach out and accept his hand and tell him that she did forgive him. At that moment, it was like the venom and hatred flowed out of her. "It was God's love flowing through me to him," she told me. "I really did release him from what he had done to me. And as I did, I was set free!"

As parents we can help teach our children that principle. First, a child can begin to recognize that *the person who has offended him has problems of his own.* Everyone who offends us has his own difficulties or unmet needs. He may have low self-worth. He may feel rejected, or guilty, or resentful toward someone. As soon as we start recognizing this, we start being free in our heart and our spirit can begin to open toward that person.

Second, *we can make a commitment to pray for someone who has offended us.* When our children were young, we lived in the Chicago area. When we went through the toll booths on the expressway, our children would sometimes hand the attendants the money. They would reach over my shoulder to do so, but now and then the coins would drop and I would have to open the door to retrieve them. Some of the attendants became very irritated. As we would pull away, the children often commented about their anger. "You know why that person was mad at us?" I asked. "It's because he has an 'owwie' in his heart. That's his way of saying, 'Would someone please understand me?' " Sometimes we would pray for an attendant, which helped the children realize they shouldn't take someone else's anger personally.

The biggest problem is that people take offenses far too personally. Usually people are offensive because they have their own problems. Maybe they didn't get enough sleep, they've had a bad day, or someone at home or work has rejected them. There are any number of reasons why people can be offensive, and the sooner we recognize this, the less chance we have of being offended and having our spirit closed. However, even if it does close, we can begin to open it by recognizing that the offender has problems. Even if we never get a chance to help the offender with his problems, just wanting and intending to help many times is enough for God to open our spirit and clear our heart of resentment.

How Open Is Your Child's Spirit?

Test yourself with each of your children to see how open their spirits are. This is a simple, general evaluation that can help a parent detect whether or not a child's spirit is closing. Score each question from one to five. 1 = never; 2 = seldom; 3 = sometimes; 4 = usually; 5 = always.
1. Does my child (age two and above) enjoy touching me? _____
2. Does my child spontaneously touch me when I first see him after school or at home? _____
3. Does my child respect what I respect in life? _____
4. Does my child generally appreciate what I value in life—i.e., the Bible, my vocation, etc.? _____
5. Would my child's friends be my choice for him? _____
6. Does my child wear clothing and hairstyles that I approve of? _____
7. Does my child choose the activities I would choose for him? _____

8. Does my child's music reflect what I approve of?

   _____

9. Does my child enjoy having conversations with me?

   _____

10. Does my child agree in general with my opinions?

    _____

11. Does my child enjoy going places with me? _____
12. Does my child obey me regularly? _____
13. Does my child generally reflect a warm affection for me? _____
14. Does my child naturally enjoy looking into my eyes?

    _____

Total Score _____

These scores may indicate:
14–20—Danger, resolve immediately.
21–30—Warning, proceed with caution.
31–40—Watch out for falling rocks.
41–50—Things may be bumping along, but o.k.
51–70—End of Construction. Drive carefully.

If you believe that one or more of your children are closing or have closed their spirits toward you, one effective way to start reopening their spirits is to take them out to dinner or get away for a weekend. During that time, let the child know you are trying to have the best relationship with him that you can. Then mention a particular incident that you think offended him and ask him if it did. If it didn't, you can ask, "If that wasn't it, what are some things _you_ can think of that I have done in the past that have really hurt you?" Be prepared, however, to hear something that you do not expect. As offenses surface from the past, simply do the same things you would do with an immediate offense. Go through all five steps—being soft, understanding, admitting you were wrong, trying to touch, and seeking forgiveness.

84 Ways We Can Offend Our Children

As you seek to discover how you might have offended your child, you may need some help coming up with possibilities. In my counseling and work with children around the country, I have asked many of them how their parents have offended them. I took their answers and compiled them. Here are their actual responses:

1. Lacking interest in things that are special to me.
2. Breaking promises.
3. Criticizing unjustly.
4. Allowing my brother or sister to put me down.
5. Misunderstanding my motives.
6. Speaking carelessly.
7. Punishing me for something for which I already had been punished.
8. Telling me that my opinions don't really matter.
9. Giving me the feeling that they never make mistakes.
10. Not being gentle when pointing out my weaknesses or blind spots.
11. Lecturing me and not understanding when all I need is some support.
12. Never telling me "I love you." Never showing me physical affection.
13. Not spending time alone with me.
14. Being insensitive, rough, and breaking promises.
15. Being thoughtless.
16. Never telling me "thank you."
17. Not spending time together.
18. Being insensitive to my trials.
19. Speaking harsh words.
20. Being inconsistent.
21. Being taken for granted.
22. Being told how to do something that I was doing on my own.

23. Nagging me.
24. Bossing me.
25. Feeling unnoticed or unappreciated.
26. Being ignored.
27. Not being considered a thinking and feeling person.
28. Being too busy to care for me and listen to me.
29. Dismissing my needs as unimportant, especially when their work or hobby is more important.
30. Bringing up old mistakes from the past to deal with present problems.
31. Teasing excessively.
32. Not noticing my accomplishments.
33. Making tactlesss comments.
34. Liking me only for my physical looks or abilities, instead of what's inside me.
35. Not being praised and appreciated.
36. Being built up and then let down.
37. Getting my hopes up to do something as a family and then not following through.
38. Being corrected without being reminded that they love me.
39. Being disciplined in harshness and anger.
40. Not reasoning with me, and never giving me an explanation of why I'm being disciplined.
41. Misusing brute force.
42. Reacting to me in the opposite way I think a Christian should treat me.
43. Raising their voices to each other.
44. Not being interested in who I am.
45. Cutting down something I am doing or someone I am with as being dumb or stupid.
46. Using foul language when they are upset with me.
47. Being impatient, which often comes across as rudeness.
48. Saying "no" without giving a reason.

49. Not praising me.
50. Sensing a difference between what is said with the mouth and what is said through facial expressions.
51. Making sarcastic remarks about me.
52. Making fun of my hopes, dreams, and accomplishments.
53. Punishing me severely for something that I didn't do.
54. Being distracted when I really have something to say.
55. Insulting me in front of others.
56. Speaking before thinking through how it will affect me.
57. Pressuring me when I already feel low or offended.
58. Comparing me with other kids at school and telling me how wonderful they are and that they wish I could be better.
59. Forcing me to argue with them when I'm really hurt inside.
60. Being treated like a little child.
61. Not approving of what I do or how I do it. I keep trying to get their approval but they just won't give it.
62. Seeing them do the very things they tell me not to do.
63. Ignoring me when I ask for advice because they are too busy.
64. Ignoring me and not introducing me to people who come to the house or we see in public.
65. Showing favoritism toward my brother or sister.
66. Acting as if something I want is of little importance.
67. Not feeling like I am special to them. It's so important to me to have my parents let me know, even in small ways, that I'm special to them.
68. Seeing my father put my mother down, especially in front of company.
69. Seldom touching or holding me.

70. Hearing mom and dad bickering at each other to the point where one of them is really hurt.
71. Not trusting me.
72. Making fun of something physically different about me.
73. Seeing my mom and dad trying to get revenge against each other.
74. Sensing that my dad never approves of what I do or how I do it.
75. Not being able to control their anger.
76. Getting mad at me because I can't keep up with their schedule or abilities.
77. Making me feel like they wish they never had me in the first place.
78. Not having enough time for me.
79. Needing my parents but they are glued to the television.
80. Seeing my parents spend a lot of money on their pleasures, but when I want something, they don't seem to have the money.
81. Making me feel childish.
82. Not spending the time to understand what I am trying to say.
83. Yelling at me when I already know I'm wrong.
84. Making me feel like I hadn't tried to improve at something when I really had.

2

Parenting for Positive Results

- *Four Basic Types of Parenting:*
  The Dominant Parent
  The Neglectful Parent
  The Permissive Parent
  The Loving and Firm Parent
- *The Two Most Important Factors in Raising*
  Children

My heart sank when I saw the police car pull into our driveway. I knew why it was there. Too scared to move, I sat still, trying to look innocent while my mother opened the door.

The officer introduced himself, then turned to me. "Have you been with your friend Jimmy today?" he asked.

"Yes," I said, trying my best to hide my nervousness. "I see him all the time."

"Were you down at the river with him?"

"No. I wasn't anywhere near the river."

The officer looked at my mother and then back at me. "Jimmy told me you were down there with him. He also said that the two of you broke into one of the homes there."

I could feel the blood rushing to my face as I shook my head in denial. The officer kept talking: "You're going to have to appear at juvenile court next week. I'll have witnesses there."

I began to cry and then admitted everything. "I was down at the river. We did break into a house. But we only took a couple of small items."

This wasn't my first brush with trouble. A few of the town merchants had accused me of stealing money and items from their stores. I hadn't stolen anything from them, but my reputation was established, so they suspected me anyway. There were rumors going around town that I probably would be sent to reform school. Growing up, I basically did what I wanted to do when I wanted to. I'm sure that I deserved hundreds of spankings for my actions and irresponsible attitude as a child, but my parents never once disciplined me. As a result, there have been many areas where I have had difficulty adjusting as an adult. For one thing rules never apply to me. If a sign says "no parking," I may park anyway because "I'm an exception." Because there were no rules in my home, I figured rules were for others, not me.

However, the attitude of my parents did have one very positive result in my life; it laid the foundation for a strong sense of self-worth. This fact could sound strange after reading about all of the trouble I was involved in. But as I look back to how I was raised, I can see that my parents were one of four types of parents we'll discuss in this chapter. I now understand how I was able to grow up with a positive self-image in a home void of discipline.

A few years ago, Dr. Dennis Guernsey described four basic categories of parents in an article for *Family Life Today*. His observations were based on a study by three Ph.D.s at the University of Minnesota. Two types of parents tend to cause their children to resent authority. These children tend to dislike themselves. They may do poorly in school and are often convinced that they never will be successful. These same two types of parents also tend more frequently to close the spirit of their children, resulting in the various problems we mentioned in chapter 2.

The other two categories of parents—one of which characterized my mother and father—tend to produce more positive-acting children. These children are more secure and tend to like themselves. They do better in school and are more responsible as adults.

As we examine each type of parent, it is important not only to examine the kind of parents we would like to be, but also to evaluate our lives in light of how we were parented.

Four Basic Types of Parenting

1. The Dominant Parent. This type of parent tends to produce the most negative qualities in children. Dominant parents usually have very high standards and expectations. But they seldom offer warm, caring support and very few explanations are given for their rigid rules. They tend to be unbending and demand that their children stay away from certain activities because of their strong convictions. But because the children do not know the reasons why these activities are wrong, they may secretly participate in them.

A group of psychologists and psychiatrists studied 875 third graders in rural Columbia County, New York, from 1960 to 1981 and made several conclusions concerning dominant parents. They found that high aggression in younger children is caused by the actions of overly dominant parents. This high aggression usually lasts a lifetime and can lead to major violence. The study also showed that harsh punishment, like washing out children's mouths with soap, coupled with rejection can lead to aggressive behavior.

These are some typical statements and actions by dominant parents:
- "Rules are rules. You're late—to bed with no dinner."
- "I won't stand for your back talk. Apologize." (Or slap the child's face.)
- "You don't need reasons. Just do what I say."
- "I don't care how many of your friends will be there. You're not going and I don't want to hear another word about it, do you hear?"
- "No son of mine is going to goof off. You took the job; you get it done."
- "How many times have I told you to stop that? Get in there—you're going to get it!"

These are some possible reactions by children who have dominant parents:
- They rank lowest in self-respect. They have little ability to conform to rules or authority.
- The rigid harshness of the parent breaks the spirit of the child and results in resistance, "clamming up," or rebellion.
- The child usually does not want anything to do with his parents' rules or values. He tends to reject the ideals of his parents.
- The child may be attracted to other children who rebel against their parents and the general rules of society. They may use drugs and participate in other illegal activities.
- The child may be loud and demanding of his rights.
- In a classroom setting, he may cause disruption in order to gain attention from others.

2. The Neglectful Parent. Neglectful parents tend to lack both loving support and control over their children. They show an uncaring or immature attitude, lashing out at a child when pushed or irritated. These parents tend to isolate themselves from their children by excessive use of babysitters and to indulge in their own selfish activities. Children are viewed as a bother, "to be seen and not heard."

Dr. Armand Nicholi, psychiatric professor at Harvard Medical School, helped me understand that neglectful parents are not only absent when they are away from home. They rob their children of one of the most important factors in their lives—emotional accessibility. When they are home, they usually are not listening or paying attention to their children.

There are four main reasons why our children are being neglected today, according to Dr. Nicholi:

a. *The high divorce rate.* Statistics show that there are more than thirteen million children in single parent homes. The divorce rate has been upwardly spiraling since the early 1960s and has increased 700 percent since the beginning of this century. Most divorces require single parents to work outside the home, allowing less time for the emotional development of their children. It's very difficult for single parents to provide their children with the necessary time each day for listening and emotional accessibility. However, it's not impossible.

b. *The increase of mothers in the work force.* More than 50 percent of all mothers in the United States are working. This also greatly increased in the 1960s, with a strong emphasis being put forth that women were unfulfilled in their homes. The economic pressures of the times also forced many women to seek jobs. By joining the work force, mothers are often less accessible to their children.

The suicide rate among children ages ten to fourteen has tripled in the last ten years. Dr. Nicholi says this can be directly related to changes in the American home. One study he quoted shows that American parents spend less time with their children than parents in any other nation except England. The study quoted one Russian father who said he would not even think of spending less than two hours daily with his children. In contrast, a study at Boston University found that the average father in the United States spends about thirty-seven seconds a day with his children.

c. *Excessive television viewing.* This also increased greatly in the sixties and now more than 90 percent of American homes have at least one TV. The problem with television is that even though people are physically together in a room, there is very little meaningful and emotional interaction. As parents neglect their children by watching television or through other activities, the children experience an emotional loss similar to that of losing a parent through death. They often feel guilty when their parents are not with them. Some even believe the reason is because they are bad, and if only they were better, their parents would spend more time with them. Obviously, this awareness lowers a child's sense of worth.

d. *An increasingly mobile society.* More than 50 percent of Americans change addresses every five years. This mobility robs children of their parents' time as well as the emotional strength and accessibility they have from friends and relatives in their former home. Yet even if we have to move our families, we can still provide emotional accessibility to our children. This can be done by setting aside time every day to spend with each of our children or together as a family. Dr. Nicholi stressed that this time should be used to counteract the effects of our mobile society.

To illustrate how prevalent the problem of emotional accessibility is, take a short break and try spending just five minutes concentrating on your family's welfare and how you can help meet each child's emotional needs. You may find it very difficult because we're not used to doing this in our culture.

Listed below are some typical actions and statements made by neglectful parents:

- "Work it out by yourself. Can't you see I'm busy?"
- "No! I'm expected somewhere else tonight. Get your mother to help you."
- "No, you can't stay up. Remember you wanted to stay up late last night. Stay out of my hair!"
- "That's your problem. I've got to get to work."
- "Good grief! Can't you kids be more careful?"
- "Late again, for heaven's sake. Would someone please pass the meat?"
- "So you think I'm stupid, huh? Well, that's your problem, buddy. Just get lost!"

Here are some possible effects on children of neglectful parents:

- The harshness and neglect tend to wound the spirit of a child, resulting in rebellion.
- The neglect teaches the child that he is not worth spending time with.
- The child develops insecurity because his parents are never predictable.
- The child may not develop a healthy self-respect because he is not respected and has not learned to control himself.
- Broken promises break the spirit of the child and lower his self-worth.
- The child tends to do poorly in school, because he has little motivation.

3. The Permissive Parent. Permissive parents tend to be warm, supporting people, but weak in establishing and enforcing rules and limits for their children.

This was the type of parents that I had. My mother and father were very warm and loving and accepting of me. But as far as I can remember, there were no rigid rules in our home. They usually gave in to my demands. Even when I was in trouble, they would not spank or discipline me. My mother said she never spanked because her first child died of blood poisoning and she had spanked her two weeks before she died. She made my father promise to never spank any one of their five remaining children.

Although they meant well, that leniency affected me negatively. My parents left all decisions concerning how I would spend my spare time up to me. In fact I didn't start formally dating until . . . the third grade! This caused a number of problems in my life. Once my father caught me in a serious infraction as a young boy. From his firm voice I knew that I was in trouble. But later, he said he would let me off without punishing me if I promised not to do it again. I actually told him that I needed a spanking but he wouldn't do it. There was something in me that wanted to be corrected.

I found the same permissiveness in school. Once a teacher caught me passing notes in the third grade after warning me of the consequences if I didn't stop. She sent me to the principal. He talked to me for awhile, told me I needed to shape up, then said that he was going to spank me. I thought he really meant business, but about fifteen minutes later, he said he was going to give me another chance if I promised not to pass notes again. Of course, I promised the world, but inwardly I can remember being disappointed that he didn't follow through.

One of the major reasons why some parents are too permissive is an inner fear that they may damage their children if they are too strict. That fear of confronting their children may actually produce the very things they fear.

On the positive side, permissive parents are strong in the area of support. I am very grateful that my parents showed me warmth and love. They were very giving, very understanding, very comforting. Effective parents realize that a certain degree of permissiveness is healthy. That means accepting that kids will be kids, that a clean shirt will not stay clean for long, that children will run instead of walk, and that a tree is for climbing and a mirror for making faces. It means accepting that children have the right to childlike feelings and dreams. That kind of permissiveness gives a child confidence and an increasing capacity to express his thoughts and feelings.

Overpermissiveness, on the other hand, allows for undesirable acts such as beating up other children, marking on buildings, and breaking objects.

The following statements and actions are typical of permissive parents:

- "Well, O.K. You can stay up late this time. I know how much you like this program."
- "You're tired, aren't you? A paper route is a tough job; sure, I'll take you around."
- "I hate to see you under all this pressure from school. Why not rest tomorrow? I'll say you're sick."
- "You didn't hear me call you for dinner. Well, that's all right. Sit down. I don't want you eating a cold dinner."
- "Please don't get angry with me. You're making a scene."
- "Jimmy, please try to hurry. Mommy will be late again if we don't start soon."

These are possible reactions by children who have permissive parents:

- A child senses that he is in the driver's seat and can play the parent accordingly.
- A child develops a feeling of insecurity, like leaning against a wall that appears to be firm, but falls over.

- A child may have little self-respect because he has not learned to control himself and master certain personal disciplines.
- A child learns that because standards are not firm, he can manipulate around the rules.

4. The Loving and Firm Parent. Loving and firm parents usually have clearly defined rules, limits, and standards for living. They take time to train their children to understand these limits—like why we don't carve love notes on the neighbor's tree—and give clear warnings when a child has transgressed an established limit. But they also give support by expressing physical affection and spending personal time listening to each child. They are flexible, willing to listen to all the facts if a limit has been violated.

The loving and firm parent is a healthy and balanced combination of the dominant and permissive parents. There is firmness with clearly defined rules like, "You cannot intentionally harm our furniture or anyone else's," but this firmness is combined with loving attitudes and actions.

Here are some typical statements and actions by loving and firm parents:

- "You're late again for dinner, Tiger. How can we work this out together?" (Parents spend time working out solutions with the child.)
- "Hey, I wish I could let you stay up later, but we agreed on this time. Remember what you'll be like tomorrow if you miss your sleep?"
- "When we both cool off, let's talk about what needs to be done."
- "You're really stuck, aren't you? I'll help you this time. Then let's figure out how you can get it done yourself next time."
- "You say all the other girls will be there. I'd like to have more information first."

- "Did you do your piano? I hate to do this, but we agreed—no dinner before it is finished. We'll keep it warm for you."
- "You may answer the phone, but before you answer, you must learn to answer it the right way."

Typical characteristics of children who have loving and firm parents:

- The warm support and clearly defined limits tend to build self-respect within the child.
- A child is more content when he has learned to control himself.
- His world is more secure when he realizes that there are limits which are unbending, and he understands why—the underlying principles.
- Because the spirit of a child is not closed, the lines of communication are open with parents. There is less chance of the "rebellious teen years."
- The children from loving and firm parents ranked highest in: a) self-respect b) capacity to conform to authorities at school, church, etc. c) greater interest in their parents' faith in God and d) greater tendency not to join a rebellious group.

The supportive and firm parent reflects the very specific biblical instruction for parenting. It stresses two important ways that parents must take care of their children. First, they must *discipline* their children, which partly means setting clearly defined limits in the home. Second, they must follow the greatest *instruction* in Scripture—to love one another.

The Two Most Important Factors in Raising Children

I have concluded that the two most important factors in raising children are:

1) establishing clearly defined and understood rules in the home; limits that the children know they cannot violate without some consequence.

2) a commitment to love each child in a warm, affectionate, and supportive way.

In the chart below, each of these four types of parents is summarized. The dominant parents are lower in their ability to show loving, warm support and higher in the establishment of rigid rules and limitations. Neglectful parents have a tendency to be lacking in warm and loving support and also in establishing rules and limits around the house. Permissive parents have a greater tendency to be loving, warm, supportive and approving, yet lack the ability to establish clearly defined limits and rules. The fourth type of parent, the loving and firm parent, has established clearly defined limits and is more diligent in communicating warmth and loving support.

Parents	Love and support for their children	Controlling children by limits or rules at home
Dominant	Low	High
Neglectful	Low	Low
Permissive	High	Low
Loving and Firm	High	High

3

Expressing Loving Support—The Most Important Aspect of Raising Children

- *Unconditional Commitment*
- *Scheduled Times*
- *Availability to Children*
- *Tender Treatment*
- *Frequent Eye Contact*
- *Listening in an Understanding Way*
- *Meaningful Touching*

The tension was thick in the front seat of our car. Greg stared silently out the window. "I know what you've been doing," I said. My thirteen-year-old son was involved in an activity he knew was wrong. But he couldn't admit it.

With tears streaming down his face, he said, "Dad I didn't want to tell you because I knew you'd be so ashamed of me." I held out my arms and he immediately grabbed me and began sobbing. I could feel his body relax as I told him, "No matter what you have done or ever do, remember I will always love you."

With those words, Greg was able to admit what he had been doing. As Greg sensed my love for him, he was able to relax and our communication was open. In this chapter we want to explore several ways of expressing supportive love to our children, the kind of love that builds stronger families and increases a child's sense of personal value.

Unconditional Commitment

One of the most important ways to express warmth and loving support to our children is *to make an unconditional commitment to them for life.* That's the kind of commitment that says, "You're important to me today and tomorrow, no matter what happens."

My family is reminded daily of my commitment to them. At the entryway of our home hangs a wall plaque that I made. It reads: "To Norma, Kari, Gregory and Michael, in assurance of my lifetime commitment to you."

Norma and I frequently tell our children that we love them. In many ways, we let them know that we are committed to them for their entire lives, no matter what they do. We are committed to help them be successful in whatever they want to do. We will be committed to them after they are married. We will be committed to them no matter who they marry. We will be committed no matter what happens during their marriage. We will be committed to their mates and to their children. We tell them we are always available to listen. Should they get into trouble, we will be there to help. That doesn't necessarily mean we will bail them out of a tight situation, for that may not be best for them. But they know how much we love them and that nothing can ever keep us from loving them.

Mark "Golden Boy" Frazie, a professional boxer, told me how his parents demonstrated their commitment to him. When I asked Mark who was the most encouraging person in his life, without hesitation he answered, "My dad." He told me that his father is his very best friend and always will be.

"When I was nineteen years old, I went through a real trial," Mark explained. "Some of my family resisted me and many of my relatives did not understand. But my dad told me that even though he was hurt by what I had done, I was his son. He would always love me and always be there to pick me up."

In contrast, lack of unconditional commitment can result in major conflict. A frightened eighteen-year-old boy standing in front of a stern judge listened as the judge, a close personal friend of the boy's father, told him that he was a disgrace to the community and his family: "You ought to be ashamed of yourself, disgracing your family's name, causing your parents a great deal of anguish and embarrassment. Your father is an upright citizen in this community. I have personally served on numerous committees with him and know of his commitment to this city. I count your father as a close personal friend and it is with deep grief that I have to sentence you this day for your crime."

With his head bowed in obvious embarrassment, the young man listened to the judge. Then, before sentence was passed, he asked if he could speak: "Sir, I do not mean to be disrespectful or to make excuses for my behavior. But I envy you a great deal. You see, there were many days and nights that I wanted to be my father's best friend. There were many times when I needed his help with school work, in some of my dating situations, and in some of the difficult times that I faced as a teenager. But my father was gone a great deal, probably on some of those committees with you, or playing golf. I've always felt like other things were more important to him than I was. I don't mean this disrespectfully, but I truly wish I knew my father like you do."

Stunned by the boy's words, the judge placed him on probation and ordered that the boy and his father were to spend time together every week, getting to know each other. The father obviously was humiliated by the sentence, realizing his lack of commitment to his son, but it caused him to get to know his son better and that was the turning point in his son's life.

Scheduled Times

A second way that we as parents can show our love is to *schedule special times with the family.* Communicating warm, loving approval to our children doesn't just happen naturally. I believe this time should be scheduled on a regular basis—preferably daily—because our children need us.

Schedule times that are meaningful for all persons involved. The activity itself is not so important, but it does need to be something that is enjoyable for both the child and the parent. Often the deepest relationships can be developed during the simplest activities.

As a family, we camp together frequently. It is during those times in the car, lying in our sleeping bags, or waiting for a fish to bite when things are said that give us a deep understanding about our children. These special times help us understand where they are going in life and what concerns them. Just being with them communicates they are loved. A parent's willingness to wait for conversation to develop further amplifies their child's self-worth.

One summer night we were in our motor home driving from Portland, Oregon, to Chicago. It was about 10:00 P.M. and everyone was asleep. I had planned to stop at a campsite around 11:00, but Kari, who was about thirteen years old at the time, was awakened and wandered up front and sat next to me. She brought up the subject of dating and marriage and we got involved in a most meaningful discussion about the consequences of premarital sexual involvement. We had no place to go. There was no telephone to interrupt us. There is no way I could have planned a more meaningful time together. We didn't need to stop for food. And she was, of course, highly interested in the conversation. We stayed up until 2:00 A.M. while everyone else slept. These times seldom occur unless we plan time together. If our children see us neglect other things to spend time with them, they will realize how important they are to us.

I often wonder why we, as parents, are so reluctant to tell our children how valuable they are to us. We need to let them know regularly that they are tremendously important to us. On a scale from zero to ten, where do your children feel they rate in importance to you? My children know that they are about a nine to me. They are the most important things in my life other than my relationship with God and my wife. Sometimes I allow their value to drop to a four or seven, but I keep pushing it back up to nine with a conscious decision to value them. Gloria Gaither and Shirley Dobson have written a book called *Let's Make a Memory*. It is a super resource, filled with ideas for things to do during scheduled times for parents and children.

Availability to Children

Besides unconditional commitment and scheduling meaningful times together we need to *communicate that we are available* to our children both during scheduled and unscheduled times. Sometimes when I'm reading the paper, watching something special on TV or heading out the door for a meeting, one of my children will walk up and say, "Dad, you got a minute? I've got this problem in geometry." Or Kari might say, to Norma in the kitchen, "Mom, what am I going to do? I can't find anything to wear." We must be careful what we communicate at these times. If we say, "Not now, I'm busy," they'll observe what we are doing and compare their importance to it. Often we can say, "Now isn't a good time to talk, but I can give you my undivided attention in thirty minutes." Sometimes we can drop what we're doing, because our children are simply more important.

Children might go a whole day without asking for our help. But as Dr. Campbell explains in his book, *How to Really Love Your Teen-Ager*, teens have something like a "container" built within them and every once in a while they run out of "emotional gas." This is when they come up and need to be close to us. They need touching, listening, understanding, and our time. After we have filled their "emotional gas tank" they usually say, "Well, see you later." Maybe we haven't finished everything we wanted to say, but they're filled up. And that's o.k. I want my children to know they are valuable and that I am available most of the time when they need me.

Being available does not mean that we wait around for our children. It does mean evaluating what is most important to us in life. Is it needlepoint? Golf? Television? Football? Work? How many parents would say that the newspaper is more important than their children? Probably none. Yet many parents appear to be unavailable or even become angry if their children approach them with some special need while they are reading.

It is natural for a father to become engrossed in his work, but a man must evaluate why he is working. Is he primarily working to meet the needs of his family or to meet his own needs? If he is working to meet the needs of his family, he should not rationalize that it is o.k. to spend many extra hours at work because he is feeding his children or preparing to send them to college. In reality, kids have a much greater need for *time with dad*, than knowing dad is away at work so they can eat or attend college.

Because I can easily get involved with my vocation and rationalize time away from my children, I reevaluate on a regular basis. I often ask my wife if she feels I am spending enough time with our children. I also ask our children the same question, carefully listening to what they say.

Children don't expect that parents give up all of their activities and fun times just so that they are always available for them. But they must see that these other activities are not as valuable as they are to their parents.

Tender Treatment

Another aspect of communicating love to children is how parents act while with them. *Children need to be treated tenderly.* Gentleness and tenderness are of prime importance in dealing with our children. Harshness and angry lecturing communicate to children that they are of little value and in some cases worthless. The phrase "If I meant anything to anyone, they wouldn't be so mean to me" is the frequent subconscious conclusion teens draw.

The calming effect of tenderness in a home has tremendously positive effects. Sometimes, while I'm reading in the evening, one of my kids will climb up on my lap. They may want to talk; other times they're content just to be with me. It's not unusual for Kari to come to me and say something like, "Dad, I'm having a problem with a friend at school. Do you think we could talk about it tonight?" She knows that I am usually open to that situation. And I have learned that when we do get together, she wants me to listen, remain calm, offer some suggestions, and especially try to understand her suggestions. She does not want or need a lecture. Above all, she wants me to be tender while I'm listening.

Recently I violated almost every principle I recommend in this book, but because Kari, now seventeen years old, knows I love her and our relationship is strong, it appeared that she was just barely affected by my insensitivity. Under the stress of finishing this book and several other major responsibilities I launched into a firm and serious lecture with her. "Don't you ever wait until the last day to finish a school report," I ranted. I threatened her social life and anything else that came to mind. I left the house with a close friend and halfway through dinner I excused myself and telephoned Kari. "Kari," I said, tenderly and apologetically, "Dad was wrong, wasn't he?" Often I think children are much more mature than their parents. She answered, "Dad, Mom explained the pressures you are under. The reason I never answered you was because I knew what you're going through. Thanks for calling though, I love you."

In the heat of a family argument I can forget all about being tender. I'm particularly vulnerable when I return home from a trip and am physically and emotionally exhausted. On one such day, Kari said she wanted to participate in some athletic activity but didn't know which one to choose. She had mentioned this on several occasions but never followed through on any of my suggestions. This time, I suggested she go out for track at school. She told me she had no interest in track. That angered me. "I want you to go out for track," I yelled. "If I tell you to go out for track, that means you're going out for track!" She was shocked by my response. Here she was, sixteen years old, a lovely girl with a great attitude, and I was upset because she wasn't going out for track. I knew I was wrong. I could see I was closing her spirit. But I was too upset to deal with it right then.

In situations such as this, it is often best to leave the conflict for awhile. Later that evening, when I'd calmed down, I gently approached Kari. (This was after I had made a deal with my family. Because they are all extremely valuable to me, I had told them I would give ten dollars to anyone if I ever took out my frustrations on him.) I felt so bad about what I'd said to my daughter, I made out a check to her for twenty dollars. I knocked on Kari's door and heard her say very hesitantly, "Who is it?" When I told her it was me, she said, "Oh, Dad, I can't take any more of this right now."

When I told her I needed to talk with her, she unlocked the door. I handed her the check, explaining, "Kari, I know this doesn't buy your love, and it doesn't get me off the hook. But what I did to you was very wrong, and you're too valuable to be treated that way. I want to give you this little gift."

A smile broke across her face and she was a little embarrassed. "Oh, Dad, you don't have to do this." I could tell that her spirit was opening as we spoke. Even if I hadn't given her anything, but had gently apologized, it would have helped begin the process of opening her spirit. When I gave her the money—twice the amount I agreed to give her—I was communicating in a small way how valuable she was to me.

It is easier for me to do this today, because I have been practicing for several years. However it wasn't easy at first. If you are not used to being tender and admitting wrong actions as a parent, it will be difficult for you to humble yourself. But it will pay valuable dividends in the lives of your children.

Frequent Eye Contact

Children need frequent eye contact with us. Frequent eye contact is a very effective way of communicating love to anyone. This can also help a parent evaluate whether or not a child's spirit is closing. A child whose spirit is closing tends to look down or away, or turn his entire body away from the parent. With younger children, it helps to get down on our knees and look them straight in the eye.

I've often heard Norma say, "Now, look me in the eyes," when questioning our children. She says that she can usually sense whether a child is telling the truth. It is difficult for a child to keep his eyes on his parents when he is guilty. He looks down, or away, or his eyes begin to blink. A child may confess something just because of our gentle insistence that we look each other in the eyes.

Listening in an Understanding Way

The sixth aspect of communicating love to our children is *listening in an understanding way.* Listening is one skill that many people take for granted. However, I believe listening is so important that I recommend parents purchase a book or enroll in a course on how to listen. Listening does not come naturally. Most adults are preoccupied with their own needs and problems and therefore have a tendency not to listen carefully to those around them. By not noticing the needs of others, we can communicate that we are not interested in them.

There are several important points to remember about being an effective listener with our children:

A good listener desires *eye contact* with the speaker. That means stopping our activities—putting the newspaper down, turning the television off—and giving our undivided attention.

A good listener *never assumes he knows what the other person is saying.* I have reacted to something one of my children said only to learn later that what I understood wasn't what he really meant. One of the fastest ways to close a person's spirit is to accuse him of something that he doesn't really mean.

I have found it helpful to ask questions to clarify what the other person has said. *I repeat in different words what I think they mean.* Then I ask them, "Is that what you are saying?" If they say, "Well, Dad, that's close, but that's not quite it," I say, "Well, we have plenty of time. Just what do you mean by that?" Then they will repeat what they are trying to tell me.

Greg is our resident comedian. But one time I thought he took it too far when I found Michael, at age three, lying on the bottom of a motel swimming pool. After rescuing Mike, I rushed him to our room so a local doctor could check him. Greg was chasing us when he yelled, "Dad wait, I can't keep up. He's o.k., I'm sure!" and he started to laugh. I stopped, snapped my head around and scolded him, pointing for him to stay with Mom. "What does he know about the seriousness of this situation?" I muttered as I continued running. Later, Greg tried to explain what he meant. Instead of reacting, I asked him to explain himself. He simply was trying to tell me that he wanted to help and in his nervousness he began to laugh without really knowing why.

Another key factor in being a good listener is to *not overreact or take immediate action.* One day I almost ran to Kari's school after hearing what one of her teachers had said about her in class. I was extremely upset that a professional teacher would say what he said to her. Kari immediately started crying and pleaded with me that I not confront the teacher. When I saw her fear I calmed down and reassured her that I would not go to the teacher without her permission. My assurance gave her the added freedom to share the rest of what he had said.

Later, after we'd both had time to think, I asked Kari for permission to see the teacher and she granted it. Norma and I confronted him, repeating what Kari had said he shared in class about her. The teacher confessed it, apologized to us and asked if he could see Kari immediately. We took him to her and in tears he put his arms around her and sought her forgiveness. It was a special moment for all of us. Because I had not acted impulsively but instead asked for her permission first, Kari has continued to be open in sharing with us what happens in her life at school.

I have found that it is best to go through a whole conversation, then later on, after we have had time to think, take action with the agreement of the child involved. An immediate reaction causes children to fear bringing up things in the future, cutting the lines of communication.

Once I was locked in an argument with Greg concerning one of his grades. In my frustration, I said I was going to ground him from everything, forever. Kari calmly reminded me of my own commitment to wait a few days after a trip before changing or establishing a new rule that affected the kids. She was right. After a few days, I had forgotten all about the situation. Patience is crucial to building trust and openness between the parent and child.

In order to be a good listener, it is also important that we *not ridicule what our children say.* We may not understand what they are saying, but being critical or ridiculing a child lowers his sense of worth and can cut off meaningful communication.

In his book, *The Family That Listens,* Dr. H. Norman Wright outlines some additional ideas about listening:

1. Parents must be careful not to stereotype children. If you feel your child is a complainer, a whiner, a bully, or procrastinator, it may affect what you think he is saying. If we think, "Oh, he's just a whiner, it's not important what he says," we may miss learning some vital information.

2. People tend to listen five times as fast as another person can speak. If your child talks at one hundred words per minute, and you can listen at five hundred words per minute, what do you do with the remainder of time? Often boredom sets in and we daydream. Or we try to help our

children express their thoughts rather than taking the time to listen to what they really mean.

3. We need to listen with our entire body, not just our ears and eyes. We cannot listen effectively as we walk away, fix dinner, or flip through the paper. We listen most effectively with our body turned toward the speaker, leaning slightly forward.

Each of these areas: *unconditional commitment, scheduled time, availability, tender treatment, frequent eye contact,* and *listening in an understanding way* increases our children's sense of worth and value. As they feel more valued, they feel loved.

Meaningful Touching

The last major way we express love for our children is through *meaningful touching.* There is a great deal of research emerging about the importance of touching and hugging our children.

According to some research, the skin is the largest organ of our body and has a built-in need to be touched. Physiologists contend that the nerve endings of the skin actually are associated with certain vital glands centered in the brain. These glands regulate growth and many other important functions of the body. Research suggests that some children, because of a lack of touching, actually have their growth stunted to some degree. At the University of Minnesota, they have what is called "hugging therapy sessions," where the nurses and attendants spend time hugging and touching neglected children in a meaningful way while telling them they are doing great. Researchers found that these children actually caught up with their peers in physical growth.

In addition to stimulating their growth and aiding their physical health, touching also communicates to children that they are valuable. When I place my hand tenderly on my child's shoulder, I am actually communicating, "You are important to me. I want to spend time with you." On the other hand, pushing our children away or hitting them with our hands communicates rejection. Refusing to touch our children communicates to them that they are "untouchable." Our touching must be meaningful from the child's point of view in order to be effective.

For a wife, a type of meaningful touching from her husband is when he holds her tenderly during a conversation. To find out whether his touch is meaningful to her, a husband can ask his wife. The same is true with children. We can actually ask them, especially as they grow older, if we are too rough, or if we touch too frequently or not enough.

It is important to remember that touching is a two-way street. Not only is it essential for parents to touch their children, but also for children to touch their parents. It is important for children to know that their parents need to be hugged. We don't depend on their hugs and touches like they do ours, but they may not realize that we have the same emotional and physical needs and we appreciate the spontaneity of their affection.

Once we were having our regular family meeting and the discussion turned to touching. During the conversation, we mentioned to Greg, who was fifteen years old, that we needed him to respond when we tried to hug him. He looked embarrassed, so we talked further about it. He said that he didn't realize that by resisting some of our hugs we were feeling that he didn't like us. He changed immediately and became much more receptive to our hugs, even though at times we feel he is trying to rearrange our backbones.

There are several types of touching that are appropriate with children: holding them in our laps while reading to them, hugging them when they arrive home from school, or just holding hands. We have a family hold, where we interlock our little fingers. Every member of our family knows that this is our special secret family tradition hold. Norma and I started holding hands like this when we were first engaged. It is a personal, physical sign of affection in our family. Obviously, as our children have grown older, we seldom hold hands with them. One of the problems in today's culture is that we have associated touching of any kind with sexual connotations. We need to realize that touching does not need to have such overtones.

A real sense of meaningfulness and security comes from touching. At times our children will stay in bed on a Saturday morning. I will go into their rooms and put my arm by their pillow and they will lay their heads on my arm. Other times I will touch them on the shoulder while we talk.

When Greg was about six, we were driving in the Chicago area, and he told me how terrible it would be if we had an accident and I was killed. I obviously agreed with him and told him I would miss him terribly. Greg looked up and melted me when he said, "You know what Dad? If you ever get killed, I want to die right with you. And I want them to put both of us in the same casket and I want to be lying on your arm." As dramatic as that was, it further illustrates how much touching our children means to them.

I haven't always been a touching person. I didn't come from a touching home. I don't recall my parents touching each other and I remember feeling uncomfortable when a relative, who liked to hug a lot, came to visit. Before we were married, I told Norma, "Now, don't expect me to be one of those 'huggy' husbands and fathers, because I'm just not like that." I had to learn over the years how to touch and enjoy it.

But touching has proven to be very meaningful because it builds a sense of value within our children. It helps meet their emotional, mental, and physical needs. To fully benefit from touching, I would say that parents should make a conscious effort to touch their children eight to twelve times a day in a way that is meaningful to them.

Expressing loving support is of paramount importance within the family structure. It is also important to remember that the *attitudes* of a parent in expressing his love are as important as *how* the love is demonstrated. We've discussed ways to express loving support to our children, and in the next chapter we will deal specifically with the second major factor in raising children—developing firm limits and understandable rules. Without the balance of love and limits, children are robbed of the wholeness God intended them to have.

4

Balancing Loving Support through Contracts

One of those rare events took place when our son Greg was about seven years old. He awakened me at 6:15 one morning, pushing on me so as not to wake Norma. "Dad, could you get up and read the Bible with me?" he whispered. What could I say? This was a special opportunity few parents could pass up.

We tiptoed downstairs and Greg sat on my lap. We began to read, trying to memorize the short verses as we read. We discussed what it meant to rejoice, give thanks, and pray, and Greg seemed quite responsive. Then we prayed together and thanked God for Greg's messy room that he had to clean up and for all the hard work facing me at the office that day. By then the whole family was up. Amazed by what they saw, they gathered around for a quick time of prayer together. Then everyone scattered and I leaned back in my chair, bathing in the joy of my son's "spiritual maturity."

A sudden racket at the top of the staircase shattered my reverie. While returning to his room, Greg gave Kari a shove against the wall. She shoved back, and the fight was on. After breaking up the combatants I couldn't help but wonder how this could happen so quickly after such a meaningful experience.

Later that week, I related this experience while speaking in another part of the country. A woman in the audience graciously said in front of the group, "Don't worry. Your children are just in one of the stages they all go through. They'll be over it in about thirty to thirty-five years."

We have watched our children go through a number of stages, some of them good, some not so good. Looking back over more than twenty years of being a family, Norma and I have concluded that through all the stages greatly valuing one another has been the most important ingredient that re-bonds us and "covers all our sins" toward each other. In other words, we have committed to love each other. Part of the meaning of love is "to attach high value or stand in awe of."

In the previous chapter we shared that we want our children to know how valuable they are to us. We try to communicate this value by spending time with them, resolving conflicts, motivating them, and keeping their spirits open. We carefully "listen" to them with our eyes. When they were younger, we got down to their level, on our knees. We take them in our arms, we touch them, we hug them, we talk with them—all to communicate the value we have placed upon them.

Shortly after we married, Norma and I made a very important decision that has affected every aspect of raising our children. We recognized that each of us was an individual, yet an equally important member of a union. Both of us had valuable skills and opinions. But, we had also committed in our wedding vows to enter into oneness. Therefore, we determined to always strive to be in agreement.

Our decision to live in agreement does not mean that one of us has to compromise or give in. Rather it means *we will resolve our disagreements so that both of us are satisfied.* This commitment has given us tremendous strength in our marriage and with our children. Sometimes it takes a while to come to a decision, but because we value each other, we are willing to work for a negotiated resolution. We agreed together when we would start having children, the names of our children, and the type of training they would receive.

Before we could resolve how to discipline our children, we needed to do our own "homework." Norma began to read various books on raising children. We interviewed parents who had raised what we believed were successful families. Norma also took a course on raising children. We began to practice what we were learning. We observed which of these ideas seemed to work and which ones the children didn't respond to or caused disharmony in our home. We were constantly adjusting our techniques as we went along.

We studied the ideas of Dr. Robert Coles, one of the nation's most influential psychiatrists. He emphasized that parents seem to have forgotten that what children need, perhaps more than anything else, are rules of life that clearly establish what is right and what is wrong—practical rules that can govern our daily lives.

We read about a survey conducted several years ago with outstanding linguists, teachers, pastors, evangelists, and medical doctors. They were asked about the influences that led to their vocational choices and why they became so successful in their respective fields. Each said he came from a strict home where there were clearly defined limits. Studies like that encouraged us to establish our own rules and discipline.

We continued to read how children need a sense of discipline and authority in their lives to help them develop emotionally and physically. It gives children a sense of security to know what their boundaries are. Much of our security in life comes from order and regularity. We are relatively confident about entering an intersection when the light is green, knowing that the light for cross traffic is red. Limits are all around us. We know that if we purchase an apple from a grocery store, it has not been injected with a deadly chemical. We can be confident that the chair we sit on will not break, the walls in our home will not collapse, and that the tires on our car, when properly taken care of, will hold air, because there are rules and limits regulating their quality. With inconsistency there is insecurity.

We read *Between Parent and Child* by Dr. Haim Ginott who agrees that children need a definite sense of limits. They need to know what is right and wrong. Dr. Ginott states that one of the greatest philosophies undermining parents has been Freud's psychoanalysis. Freud perpetuated the idea that, "I'm the way I am today because of what my parents did to me." Today's parent is uncertain about how to raise a child. He is fearful that his mistakes will have costly consequences. Therefore a parent may experience paralysis when it comes to setting limits. Dr. Ginott forced us to examine the obvious—there are certain right and wrong limits for children's behavior. These can be as simple as, "You can hit your brother with a pillow, but you cannot hit him with a hammer." This may seem simple, but we read over and over again that *it is possible, right, and essential that parents establish what is clearly defined acceptable and unacceptable behavior for their children.*

Dr. Howard Hendricks, professor at Dallas Theological Seminary and author of *Heaven Help the Home* says that parents need to set some clear objectives and priorities for their children. "You can only achieve that for which you aim," Hendricks says. "If you aim at nothing, you will hit it every time." The same goes for setting limits. If we do not have clearly defined limits, and if we change our discipline from week to week, we will not know what we're aiming at or what we want to accomplish in our discipline.

Setting Limits through Contracts

If setting limits is so important, how do parents begin?

For us, it was important to have a *basis* for deciding what is right and wrong. In our family, much of that basis comes from what we believe the Bible says about living our lives. When our children were very young, we realized that it was extremely important that we nail down what we believed to be important family limits. We were even concerned about simple things, like courtesy and table manners.

As we began selecting family limits, we knew it was important not only to set clearly defined limits, but also to have very few limits. From our studies, we came up with two fundamental concepts. They are the same two concepts that Jesus Christ claimed are the greatest commandments in life.

First, we should establish a meaningful relationship with God. This includes an understanding of what He taught about Himself in the Bible as well as how to relate to Him. Norma and I agreed that our relationship with God was the most important element of our lives, and we hoped our children would also have a relationship with Him.

The second concept followed logically from the first. We should love and value people just as we value ourselves. God gave Moses ten very specific and clearly defined commandments or limits. Each of the ten commandments is based upon the two established by Jesus in the New Testament—*valuing God and valuing people.* Jesus said that if a person lived those two commandments, he would naturally obey all the commandments in the Bible. The limits we set were based on these two principles.

When our children were around three years old, our very first and simple limits were:

1. We will obey God as we understand the Bible.
2. We will obey Mommy and Daddy.
3. We will be kind to people and things—God's creation.

With the first rule, we wanted to teach our children that we are not, as parents, the final authority. There is a higher authority. If we were to ask our children to do something that violated the Bible, we wouldn't want them to obey us. We explained to our children that we wanted to have these limits in our home because this would honor God. These were His commandments, not ours. By obeying us, they were obeying God.

The third limit naturally grew out of the first two—being kind to people and things. We didn't want to have the kids calling each other ugly names or doing anything that would make another child feel devalued. We also wanted them to learn that their brothers, sisters, and playmates were valuable because God created them.

As the children grew to six or seven, we began to revise and add to our limits. We included our children in this process and finally, years later, all five of us agree on six limits that are still in force in our home today.

Our entire contract is based on limits we have found in the Bible. We regularly remind our children that these are God's limits for our family. As they operate under the contract, they know that they are obeying God—it is God's learning process, not ours.

1. Learning to obey parents.
2. Learning to put things away after we have used them.
3. Learning to do our chores—responsibility.
4. Learning to have good manners and learning responsibility toward others.
5. Learning to take care of God's creation: people and things.
6. Learning appropriate inner character qualities.

These six limits represented our final draft of an actual written contract that each of us signed and dated. In a very real sense, this was just like any business contract. We discovered that having a written, objective contract greatly contributed to our family's harmony. It made disciplining the children so much easier because we simply pointed to the family contract, and they were much more willing to cooperate and adjust to it.

> Very simply then, discipline in our home consisted of clearly defined limits with our children. These limits became our written family contract.

Most of us live by contracts, but the majority are not written out or signed. Marriage vows and driver's licenses are contracts. Agreeing to do a certain job for an employer is a contract. There are even contracts that no one mentions. For example, you keep your yard in a certain condition or else the neighbors will complain to city officials. Drive your car eighty miles an hour and you will discover that you have a contract with the city or state and it's going to cost you a stiff fine.

The basis of a contract is that all parties participate in the negotiations. All must agree on each point and on the consequences when a point is violated. Then everyone signs the contract, putting himself under its authority.

Our children were very involved in defining the limits. For example, in our first limit, "Learning to Obey Parents," we asked them what it means to obey. They said it meant two things. First, it meant not complaining. Examples of complaining included, "Why do I have to do it? Why can't Kari do it? I'm always the one chosen. Why is it always me? Why can't you do it?"

The second part of obeying was not nagging. "Please Dad, can I do it? Can I? Please, everybody is doing it. I mean, couldn't I just do it one time?" Constant nagging was interpreted as disobedience and a violation of the command for children to obey their parents. They finally helped us define the word *obeying* to mean, "Yes, I will do it and I won't complain."

The second limit that all of us were concerned about was cleaning the house. The house was messy a great deal of the time because the kids would leave their belongings strewn about the floor. At night there was usually a stream of clothing and toys from the bathroom to their bedrooms. Together we agreed it was too much for Dad, and especially Mom, to follow them around and pick up after them. They decided that each person would learn to be responsible for his own property.

The third limitation was responsibility. We talked about the importance of each member in the family and the need to work as a unit. Everyone had responsibilities. There was homework and cleaning the bedroom and feeding the animals. Someone had to take out the trash. Piano practice was part of each child's responsibilities. Once we established all the chores that helped make our home run smoothly we felt it was important for each of us as members of the family to take an active part. This was all part of learning responsibility and sharing our part of the load.

The fourth limit was learning good manners. We defined what that meant. At meals, it meant holding silverware properly, placing a napkin on the lap, and chewing food with the mouth closed, unless of course one had wiry braces or retainers. There were also certain responsibilities for being in public. You didn't run in a grocery store or in church. You didn't crawl under a church pew and bite a sweet old lady on the ankle. *We understood that our behavior in the presence of other people was a reflection of how we valued them.*

The fifth limit dealt with taking care of God's creation—people and things. Part of taking care of God's creation is taking care of our own body. On school nights, for example, that meant the children were in bed between 8:00 and 9:00, depending on their ages. Brushing their teeth after meals was part of taking care of God's creation, as was bathing, washing hair, and wearing clean and neat clothing.

This limit also included taking care of others, such as asking questions instead of arguing. It meant trying to really understand others because what they say is important. It also included playing carefully, not hitting someone with intent to hurt, getting revenge, or calling someone a degrading name.

After writing down these first five limits into a contract (we will discuss the sixth later), we made a place for everyone to sign. If they were not old enough to sign, they scribbled in the appropriate place and I put the date next to it. This showed that we all agreed to the direction we were going to go as a family. Because we involved the children, from the earliest ages, in helping write these limits, they considered them *their* limits, rather than standards their parents were imposing on them.

We never considered any of these limits lightly. We wanted to see these five, simple limits as a part of our children's lives. That meant we had to figure out how to motivate them and what the best means of correction was when they got off course. That's when the fun began. We tried many things that didn't work before choosing a method that accomplished our goal.

Enforcing the Contract—Our Experiments

We tried spanking when one of the limits was violated. But even though spanking is very useful in discipline, it was not effective for us to regulate our family contract daily by spanking.

We tried memory exercises where Norma, the children and I all memorized the limits. I expected that after they memorized the limits, they would naturally want to follow them. It wasn't that simple.

We tried things like washing their mouths with soap if they called someone a degrading name. We only tried that a couple of times because we found it was actually degrading to the children. It was violating the very thing we were punishing them for.

We tried cutting their allowances and fining them. I had some violation tickets printed, just like a policeman would give. When they violated one of the five rules, I would write out a ticket. Fines ranged from ten to twenty-five cents, depending on the violation. It was cute for a couple of days, but it soon turned into a burden for us as parents.

The list of our punishment experiments is a long one. We tried having them write the limit they violated and how they were going to change fifty times. That was effective to a degree, but again, it only lasted a few weeks. We tried push-ups and running around the block, but both of those only accomplished the loss of weight.

We tried punishing the kids by not giving them dinner. The children thought this would be a good form of punishment because it would make them aware of how important the limits were. The first time we tried it was also the last. Greg sat about fifteen feet away from the dinner table, his tongue hanging out as we ate. Halfway through the meal, Norma said, "This is harder on me than it is on Greg." To Greg's delight, we asked him to join us.

We tried punishing by prohibiting talking, playing with toys, and staying in their bedrooms. We tried turning off the air conditioner in their rooms, no camping trips, no snacks, extra piano practice, and many others. I chuckle now as I write this. But I didn't come from a disciplined home, and there was little written about this area, so we had to experiment.

Unfortunately, nothing seemed to help our children consistently live within these five limits. Plus the methods of correction were difficult on us as parents. Sometimes it seemed like a full-time job trying to keep up with all these little rules and regulations.

In our search to discover how to implement these rules in our home, we met an outstanding pediatrician and his wife, Dr. Charles and Dorothy Shellenberger from Texas. They explained how they had implemented their limits in a practical way. It was not only effective, but provided the missing element in training our children.

A Practical Way to Implement Family Contracts

Using the contract method in a home is a very effective way to balance love and limits. Drs. Barnard and Corrales found that a family is forced to clarify limits by writing them out on paper. Before anyone is willing to sign his name, he usually desires to understand what he's putting his name to. The question then, is how to implement the contract on a daily basis.

Here's where Dr. Shellenberger greatly helped us. He taught us that there are three parts to the process:

1. *Set clearly defined limits by writing a contract.*
2. *Supervise the living of these limits regularly.*
3. *Consistently handle resistance through lost privileges.*

Number three was the missing ingredient for us. We had set limits and written the contracts, but we hadn't incorporated the violation consequences in the contract in a practical, workable way. So we gathered again as a family and reworked the contract. Since 1977, though our contract has been amended several times, the format has remained basically the same.

First, we negotiated our family contract into something like Chart #1:

Chart #1

Family Limits

1. *Learning to Obey Parents*
   Answer by saying "Yes, Dad/Mom" immediately and accomplish the request right away.
   - Do not complain: "I don't want to do that." "Do I have to?" "Can't someone else do it?" "This is not fair."
   - Do not nag: "Oh, please, please can't we do it?" "Can't I go Mom? Can't I go Mom? Can't I go Mom?"
2. *Learning to Put Our Things Away After Use*
   - Toys in our closet or garage
   - Clothes in the "dirty" box or hung up in closet
   - Towels on the towel rack
   - Have a place for everything and everything in its place
3. *Learning to Do Our Chores*
   - Clean bedroom before school
   - Place used dishes in the sink after meals
   - After school: homework and piano before play; take out trash Tuesdays and Fridays; feed cats; bring paper to Mom
   - Special chores when Mom or Dad need help

4. *Learning to Have Good Manners*
   - Meals: Walk to the table, fold hands in lap, no talking before we pray. Chew food with mouth closed, say, "Kari, please pass the _____."
   - When others are talking, wait for a pause in the conversation and say, "Excuse me Dad, could I _____?"
   - When we disagree with someone, do not say so, but rather, be a learner and ask, "What did you say again?" or "I always thought it was _____."
5. *Learning to Take Care of God's Creation: People and Things*
   People (Self):
   - 8:30 P.M.: Bath, if needed; brush teeth; put school bags by front door; read, listen to record or story
   (Others):
   - Asking questions—not arguing
   - Playing gently—not roughhousing
   - Praying for our "enemies"—not hitting
   - Being kind and sensitive—not calling names (love and kindness are gifts from God; He changes our heart)
   Things:
   - Protecting house and furniture: Not jumping and playing on chairs, beds, etc.; not throwing balls in the house or against the house; not climbing the small trees

Second, we decided as a family what lost privileges each member would have when one of the limits was violated. The children had dozens of ideas—no toys, no television, no movies, no eating out, no snacks, no dating, no telephone, no dinners for a month, being grounded. Some of their lost privileges were much harsher than we as parents would have ever put down. After we made a list of thirty or forty possible lost privileges, we went back over the list and agreed on twenty-four hours of lost privileges for each of the five limits. We revised each limit to start with the letter C; the limits came to be known as the "Five Cs." See Chart #2.

Chart #2

Our Family Limits

Responsibilities	Lost Privileges for 24 hours
1. *Conforming:* Obeying Mom and Dad—not complaining, arguing, or nagging	All toys
2. *Cleaning:* Clean room every morning; clean up after using toys or other items	Television
3. *Chores:* Lawn once a week; trash every evening; piano by 5:30 P.M.	After-school snack
4. *Courteous:* At meals; at church and outings	Joining the family the next time they eat out
5. *Caring:* To bed on time; brush teeth; kind to people and things (God's creation); not teasing, hitting, or arguing	Seeing friends

Signed: _____   Date: _____

    _____   _____

    _____   _____

    _____   _____

    _____   _____

You can see from Chart #2 that when any of our children violated one or more of the limits they might lose toys or the opportunity to watch television for twenty-four hours.

We met for ten to fifteen minutes each night after dinner to evaluate how everyone was doing in each of the five areas. We kept the chart below by the kitchen table. It was covered in plastic so we could mark on it with a grease pencil and erase it the next evening. We also used this time to correct our children rather than correct them throughout the day, unless of course they had committed a serious offense, then we would take care of it immediately.

Chart #3

Responsibilities				
	Kari	Greg	Mike	Lost Privilege
1. Conforming				toys
2. Cleaning				TV
3. Chores				snack
4. Courteous				eatout
5. Caring				friends

Responsibility is a daily decision.

This chart made keeping up with our contract simple. Each evening as we met after dinner, we would go through this chart with our children. For instance, if Greg had not been responsible with his chores that day, we would place an "X" in that square, and he would not be able to have an after-school snack the next day. He could use that time to catch up on his chores.

Don't Expect, Inspect

For three years, we met every night after dinner, applying the old Henry Brandt proverb, "People do what you inspect not what you expect." We inspected and evaluated their behavior every day. After three years we no longer met daily, because the limits had become a regular part of our children's behavior. However, the contract still serves as our Family Constitution. It is open for amendments, but we can revise it only if all five of us agree with the recommended change.

As our children entered their teen years we wrote separate contracts to include more specific areas, particularly dating and driving.

This brings us to our sixth and final limit—developing character. We added this as our children became more aware of the opposite sex. We agreed that rather than set a specific age when they could start dating, we wanted instead to see a certain level of maturity in their character. In order to define this, we again looked to the Bible. Our standards of maturity became the nine qualities found in Galatians 5:22–23, the eight beatitudes (Matthew 5:3–10), and the attitude of Christ displayed in Philippians 2:5–8. We'll list a few of the main areas that we discussed with our children.

The first area of importance was that they be able to withstand peer pressure and not compromise the standards they believed were important. Norma punctuated this by relating a story about one of her first dates in high school. She was double-dating with a girlfriend, and they had both agreed not to allow any physical contact on their first date. Norma said that all of a sudden, she looked up and noticed her friend in the arms of this new-found boyfriend. That put pressure on her. Her date began to pursue her, but Norma said "No!" When her date became angry, Norma told him to either take her home or she would walk. It took all the strength Norma could muster.

It takes a great deal of courage for a teenager to be assertive in such situations. But that is the type of character quality we wanted to see in our children before we felt they were mature enough to date.

Another inner quality we felt was important is what the Bible calls being "pure in heart." That means having a single focus on what is most important in life. We wanted our children to understand that having a solid relationship with God is essential to establishing good relationships with people.

The Bible has a certain standard for living that leads to an enjoyable life. Its limits are not designed to restrict us from happiness, but rather to keep us from certain activities that can rob us of joy and peace. For example, the Bible gives us several consequences of premarital sex. We have taught our children that sexual actions from petting on up to intercourse prior to marriage, or after marriage with someone other than our mate, have several negative results. As a family, we discovered in both religious and secular studies at least twenty negative consequences of premarital sex. Here's a sample:

- It immediately reinforces our desires for greater and more frequent sensual fulfillment.
- It reinforces our self-centered nature. As the Scriptures say, it causes us to have a hardened or calloused heart. We become less sensitive to the needs of those around us, because we spend more time looking for ways to have our own sensual needs met. We tend to observe life as a means to stimulate our own senses instead of loving those around us.
- Immorality also reduces our faith in God, because the more we violate God's limits, the more we must rationalize that "God doesn't exist" or His rules are invalid.

This can lead to questioning the very creator of those limits. Thus I've observed those who practice an immoral lifestyle have more and greater doubts about the existence of God.

- Sexual "freedom" and promiscuity can actually lead to slavery—slavery to our physical senses and impotency. A certain cigarette company has a slogan that says, "Smoke this cigarette. It satisfies." That's a clever twist of the word *satisfy*. Have you ever known a smoker who could smoke just one cigarette and be satisfied? He has to have another and then another. The same can be true with sexual immorality.

There are so many lies circulating in our world. We're told that we live in a day of sexual "freedom." Implied by the word *freedom* is the opportunity to experience sexual contact before and after marriage with a variety of partners. Just look at the inconsistency of this statement, "We're free to make love." Making love means sexual involvement and the more involved we are the more we lose our freedom to restrain our desires and the more our senses enslave us. It is important for children to understand these consequences of immorality. Even though they have strong and normal sensual drives, they must gain the ability to say "no" for their own long-term benefit and the fulfillment of lasting, loving relationships.

Contract for Dating

The first part of our dating contract deals with a child's character. The second part deals with the actual dating practice. Here are some additional elements in the dating contracts:

With the first few years of dating, we evaluate each dating situation on its own merit, but we especially favored well-organized, school-sponsored activities that were adequately chaperoned. Next, every member of the family must approve of the potential dating partner. This has been a very effective safeguard designed to protect against a potentially harmful relationship. It is a reflection of a close-knit family, each concerned about the well-being of the other.

We also discuss and set a curfew for dates. The greater a child's trustworthiness, self-control, and purity of heart, the greater freedom in dating privileges. Likewise, if any of the character qualities is tarnished or violated, then the dating privilege may be lost for an agreed-upon period of time. For example, if one of the children lies about some activity, even if it has nothing to do with dating, he may lose the privilege of dating for a week or two, depending on the severity of the offense.

We all agreed to this simple dating contract and as the children get older, we will continue to evaluate the contract. We probably will revise it a few times, which is what we encourage families to do. Stay current and up to date with children in the areas of training and correction.

Contract for Driving

Driving a car is another privilege that comes with age and character development. Even before our children were old enough to drive, we agreed as a family on the following contract:

1. Upon receiving my driver's permit, I will be allowed to drive on local errands when accompanied by either parent. I will assist in driving for extended periods of time on long family vacations under all types of driving conditions.
2. Before using the car, I will ask either Mom or Dad if I can use it and explain the purpose.
3. If I want to go somewhere for myself, both my home-

work and piano practicing or other chores must be completed first.

4. During the first month after receiving my driver's license, the radio will not be used while driving.

5. During the school year, I will be allowed to drive to activities at night but cannot take anyone home without permission.

6. I will not allow anyone else to use the car under any circumstances without permission from my parents.

7. I will not carry more than five passengers at a time.

8. I will not give rides to hitchhikers under any circumstances, and I will use extreme caution in accepting assistance if I should have difficulty with the car.

9. I will pay half of the increase of insurance costs whenever my grades fall below a B average. In case of an accident, I will assume half of the deductible costs.

10. If I receive any moving violations, I will lose my license for up to one month. On the second violation, I will lose it for up to three months.

It took us several weeks to negotiate this simple contract and our children signed it only after several revisions. We are certainly open to future revisions, but again any changes must be understood and agreed upon by each of us.

Guidelines for Spanking

Our final contract deals with the important area of spanking. Most violations of our limits are punished by a loss of privileges. But it is part of our written contract that we will use spanking if anyone is obviously resistant or rebellious, especially strong defiance against a parent.

Spanking can be very effective to guard against rebellion, but as Dr. Armand Nicholi says, the main problem with spanking is that it can be a release for the parent's frustration, guilt, or anger. It may therefore benefit the parent more than the child. He advises parents to ask themselves who will benefit most from the spanking. Spanking certainly can be used when a limit is violated, but it must be used cautiously.

I have also come to see the effectiveness of spanking on a decreasing scale. It's most effective with preschoolers, but it should rarely be used after age thirteen. If a spanking is necessary, it should be taken very seriously, so as not to close the child's spirit. Usually a loss of privileges is more effective for older children.

Before we developed our contracts, we discovered that the majority of spankings in our home took place before meals. This is often the hardest time because everyone is hungry and tired. Our blood sugar levels are low. The children are restless, impatient, and the aroma of food heightens tension. A number of things can happen at this time to flare up disobedience within children. We found I could reduce some of the tension by simply spending more time with the children when I came home from work.

We also allow our children to call for "court" if they believe that they are being disciplined unjustly by spanking. We started this after I saw Greg push a plate of chips and sandwich across the kitchen table. The plate hit Kari in the chest and the sandwich and chips went all over her and onto the floor. I immediately grabbed Greg's arm and told him, "You're going to be spanked." He was trying to tell me it wasn't his fault and Kari was trying to intervene, but I didn't pay any attention.

Only after I had spanked Greg did I gather the facts—after all I saw it happen. But I didn't know that Norma had asked Kari to make Greg a sandwich, but Greg said he wasn't hungry. Kari retorted, "Mother told me to make you this sandwich, so you're going to get it whether you like it or not." He shoved it back. The sandwich passed between the two of them at least three more times. I walked into the kitchen just as Greg was shoving it the final time out of complete frustration.

Had I taken the time to get the facts, I would not have spanked him. We initiated the court alternative to avoid similar mistakes. The defendant can call the whole family together, even call in a witness or bring in a friend to act as lawyer if he wants to present his case concerning why he believes he does not deserve this spanking. After all the facts are gathered, we go around the table asking each member of the family for his verdict. If everyone votes "guilty," we ask the person accused what he thinks. Every time we have done that, the guilty party has agreed with the others, admitting his guilt.

Here are ten factors to consider when spanking is used as a method of correction:

1. *Give clear warning before the spanking.* Children need to understand why they are being spanked. We have told our children that they must show obvious signs of rebellion against clearly established rules to get a spanking. Examples might be if they physically harm each other or if a parent tells them not to do something and they say they don't care and do it anyway.

2. *Establish a child's responsibility for his or her disobedience.* When a child disobeys after instructions and warning, the child must assume responsibility for his disobedience. We ask our children *what they have done* so they can see for themselves that they violated our family limits. Sometimes it takes a while for one to admit his wrong. He will want to blame someone else and rationalize his behavior. We must be persistent with our question until he admits what he has done wrong.

3. *Avoid embarrassment and outside interference.* When spanking or correcting a child, make sure you are alone with him, especially when the child's offense occurs in public.

If the parent brings up a problem in front of a child's friends and attempts to correct him, the child will be more concerned about his reputation than the offense he has committed. Such a correction demoralizes the child and can produce a closed spirit. It also might motivate a child to figure out ways to justify his action to those who saw him being punished so that they will side with him.

4. *Communicate parental grief over the offense.* This is important because it causes the child and parent to reflect on what has taken place. It also gives them both a chance to calm down. The ultimate goal of this time is to bring the child to a sincere repentance, where he wants to be corrected.

5. *Associate love with spanking.* It is important to explain the age-old adage, "This hurts me more than it does you," to children. My children have questioned that many times, but it is true.

Once when I was going to spank Kari, she tried to talk her way out of it. She promised never to do the offense again. She begged me not to spank her. I decided to take that opportunity to illustrate an example of real love and sacrifice.

I told her how when Christ died on the cross, He paid the penalty for our sin. Then I told her that I wanted to show her a small example of what Jesus did. I was going to let her spank me.

"Someone's going to be spanked today," I told her. "But I'm going to take your punishment for you because I love you and want you to know that I'm not spanking you to hurt you. I'm doing it because I think what you did was wrong and we are correcting it."

Kari stopped crying, her eyes lighted up and she looked at me as if to say, "Are you serious?" I told her I was, gave her the paddle and lay down on the bed just as I had asked her to do. But when she tried, she couldn't do it. I told her it was o.k., but if she didn't want to spank me, I would spank her. She quickly said that she thought she could bring herself to do it. After a long struggle, she gave me a good one. And it stung. I stood up and she gave me a big hug, like we always did with her after a spanking. This only happened once, but it gave Kari some understanding of what her parents go through.

6. *Use a neutral object for spanking.* It is important that a neutral object be used for spanking because a child has a tendency to associate the pain with the object used to spank him. If a parent uses his hand, the child may feel uncomfortable when that same hand is used to touch, hold and hug, especially if the child is spanked in harsh anger. We have found that it is very effective to use a thin stick that we decorated as a family. We call it the "teacher." Using the "teacher" also helps calm everyone because usually it takes a few minutes to find it.

The first time I used "teacher" was when Kari was about three years old. She jumped on the bed and started screaming. When I reached for her, she jumped behind the bed, then under the bed. I calmly told Kari I was going to follow through with the spanking if it took all day.

Finally, she lay down on the bed and I gave her a swat. As soon as I did, she was jumping on the bed and screaming again. I told her to lie still until I finished. So she lay down again and I gave her another swat. Again, she jumped up and started screaming. I stayed *calm,* but *firm,* and the process was repeated three more times. Finally she realized that I was serious and stayed still. Kari never jumped around like that again because she knew I meant business.

From that episode, we both learned that correction can reveal the level of a child's resistance. Persistent correction can break stubbornness, which brings us to the seventh point about spanking.

7. *Discipline or spank until the will is broken.* It is very important that we do not spank our children in harshness or severe anger, even if this means getting away for a few minutes to cool off. We must take the time to communicate love to them, but we must also communicate that we are going to spank them until they understand we mean business. If we spank children in harsh anger, it has a tendency to break their spirit, which can be worse than if we didn't spank them at all.

Once when Greg was in the seventh grade, he went through a period of blaming a poor grade in school on his teacher, his mother, even the time of day. Everyone and everything was at fault but him. I tried talking to Greg about the importance of assuming responsibility and not blaming those around him. The showdown came when Greg deliberately and willfully told me, "Dad, it's not my fault. It's their fault." He became very disrespectful to me as his father. Then I spanked him. About five minutes later, after I had spanked and hugged him, Greg sat on my lap and said, "Dad, thanks for spanking me. You know, I can see that it really is my fault." Then he sat down, got his books out and started studying. I could see the cleansing in his life because he had been corrected firmly and his stubborn will was broken.

8. *Comfort a child after the spanking.* Kari and Mike almost always crawled into my arms for a hug after a spanking. But with Greg, sometimes it took an hour or two for him to warm up and want to be touched. Once Kari and Greg chose to be spanked in the same room at the same time. They wanted to be together so they could comfort each other. They hugged each other prior to the spanking and asked who wanted to be first. They both took their spanking, they both cried, and we all hugged each other afterward. Hugging reinforces our love for the child.

9. *Discuss any restitution that might be necessary.* If a child is spanked because he hit a neighbor willfully and deliberately, it may be important for you to discuss how he should go and seek forgiveness from that neighbor. Or if he stole money from someone, you may discuss with the child how much and in what manner to repay it.

10. *Evaluate your correction and your child's response to it.* If you have wronged your child in any way, through false accusation, anger, attacking him as a person rather than his wrong behavior, embarrassing him, lacking love, or over-punishing, it is important to go to him and follow the steps of opening his spirit. This should be done when both parent and child have calmed down emotionally and can evaluate what took place more objectively. A child has a keen sense of fairness and will be highly sensitive to his parents' offenses. One of the most common accusations children have against their parents is that they rarely admit when they are wrong. This pride makes future correction very difficult because it can cause a child to close his spirit.

My worst spanking experience took place when Greg was about two years old and I tried to break what appeared to be his "strong resistant will." I wasn't swatting him hard enough to really harm him physically, but I did persist many times, trying to "break his will." As I continued I could sense his fear, frustration, and inability to explain himself. I finally stopped in grief and held him, seeking his forgiveness because I could see his resentment growing toward me. We waited until he was almost three before he received any more spankings. I felt he wasn't old enough before that to really benefit. It was, and still is, more important for us as parents to have a warm, loving relationship with our children than to have a strict "military" type atmosphere at home. The strictness is important, but I would say in training children, the emphasis should be about

45 percent strictness with limits and 55 percent a loving relationship.

Along with unconditional love and support for our children, successful parents must balance this love by establishing clearly defined rules and limits. This is the area where we had a lot to learn. And we're still learning. What I have shared in this chapter has evolved over years of trial and error.

Parenting is not something we do once and get an "A" and it's over. It would be nice if it were that easy. We must continue to learn and relearn. An NFL quarterback, Jim Zorn, told me that every year for two weeks, the quarterbacks on his team take a class where they review the fundamentals of quarterbacking. Then during preseason training camp, they practice the same techniques over and over again. The same should be true with parents. We need to continually learn, review, practice, and relearn the basics of parenting. Norma and I are still learning. Our children are ten, fifteen, and seventeen years old, but we are committed to continue learning until all of our children are raised. Then we look forward to reading, studying, and learning about how grandparents can enrich their grandchildren's lives. We hope we never stop learning.

5

Three Powerful Ways to Motivate Children

- *Use a Child's Natural Bent*
- *Use the Salt Principle*
- *Use Emotional Word Pictures*

It was 1957, in San Francisco. A tall, skinny ten-year-old boy was waiting to sneak inside Kaiser Stadium. He had waited all year for this game between the San Francisco '49ers and the Cleveland Browns and the chance to see his idol, Jimmy Brown, the all-pro running back who held almost every rushing record in the NFL. He knew that at the end of the third quarter the gate guard left and he could slip in. Even that wasn't easy for him because he had trouble walking. Raised in the ghetto, malnutrition had taken its toll and his legs were weak and bowed. He had to walk with the aid of steel splints.

After he made his way into the stadium, he stood right in the middle of the entrance to the players' tunnel, where he patiently waited for the game to end. As the final gun went off, the wiry lad struggled to stand tall so he wouldn't miss this moment. Finally, he saw Jimmy Brown turn the corner and walk toward him. As he passed by, the boy held out a piece of paper, asking politely for an autograph. Brown graciously signed it, then turned for the locker room.

But before he could get away, the boy tugged on Brown's jersey. The great running back turned and was met with this proud confession, "Mr. Brown, I have your picture on my wall. My family can't afford a TV set but I watch you on the neighbor's set every chance I get. I know what your records are and I think you're the greatest. You're my idol."

Brown put his hand on the boy's shoulder and thanked him before heading on to the locker room. But the boy reached up and tugged Brown's jersey again. Brown turned and looked into the boy's big brown eyes and asked impatiently, "Yes?"

The boy cleared his throat, held his shoulders back and head high and matter-of-factly said, "Mr. Brown, one day I'm going to break every one of your records."

Brown was so taken aback by the statement that he asked, "What's your name, son?"

The boy answered, "Orenthal James, sir. But my friends just call me O.J."

In 1973, O. J. Simpson broke Brown's long-standing single season rushing record and became the first player to gain more than two thousand yards rushing in one year. He was second behind Brown in career rushing yardage when injuries forced him to retire. Why was O. J. Simpson so motivated? Why did he have such great success?

There are many, many reasons why people are motivated—it might be the applause, the cheering of a crowd, awards—but as with O. J. Simpson, real and lasting motivation must come from within. If Simpson had viewed Jimmy Brown's records as something he never could achieve, he might have ended up in a wheelchair. But he didn't. He set a goal and believed in himself enough to accomplish that goal.

When a child uses his own energy and drive to achieve a goal he has set, he is truly motivated. That goal may be inspired by parents or friends, but it is important that the child actually set the goal and see that it is attainable and that he will benefit by reaching that goal.

Notice we stress the child setting his own goal. There is a fine line between motivation and manipulation. Dads and Moms alike need to be so careful not to use their children as pawns for their own needs. Have you ever witnessed a Dad forcing football on his son because Dad needs it—not his son?

True motivation comes from one or a combination of two factors:

1. Desire for gain.
2. Fear of loss.

Imagine waking a child on Christmas morning. He doesn't need to be motivated to get up. Eagerly he jumps out of bed because he knows there is something waiting for him. That same child will not stick his hand into a fire because he fears pain and loss, and this motivates him to avoid the flames.

Working with young children, teenagers, and college-age young people for more than thirty years has made me aware of over twenty ways to motivate children. At the heart of each of these methods is the desire for gain and the fear of loss. In this chapter, we will focus on motivating through a child's natural personality and the use of two communication tools. In the next chapter we'll cover 19 other ways to motivate children.

1. Use a child's natural bent.

I could tell that Norma was down in the dumps by her voice on the telephone. It was Mother's Day and I was away from home teaching a seminar. She was lonely and

I wished I were home. While we were talking, Greg walked into the house and presented her with a bouquet of flowers. I was pleased with his thoughtfulness, especially since he was only thirteen.

The next day I called Norma again to see how she was doing. "Oh, I'm just sitting here looking at these beautiful flowers Greg gave me," she said. I asked where Greg had gotten the flowers, hoping that he had picked them from our garden and not from the neighbor's.

"Oh, no," Norma said. "He ordered them from a florist."

"He ordered them? Where did he get the money for that?"

"Oh, he just used your charge card."

Greg is very sensitive and helpful whenever his mother is feeling down. He will vacuum the house, wash the dishes, sweep the floor—anything to make his Mom happy. But our other children respond differently, and this reflects their different personality types. Kari and Michael tend to empathize with Norma if she's feeling low; they sometimes even get discouraged along with her. But neither one tends to "kick in" like Greg does.

A person's personality type, as I'll be describing, is a result of his total physical make-up, especially his gene structures. I like to call it his "natural bent." Often there is a *combination* of personality types in a child, but usually one is predominant.

Certainly his upbringing and environment affect his "bent," but I have observed that at least five different temperaments can be found in children and it is important to understand each of them. I've arrived at these five through my observation of children through reviewing a number of studies. Each child is motivated differently, according to his or her "natural bent."

Within each of the five personality types, the behavior

of children will vary because of birth order. For example, firstborn children tend to be more pushy and prone to give orders. Secondborn children tend to be more sociable. Other factors account for variances within temperaments: being an only child, living with only one parent, being the only boy in a family of girls, and so on. Yet despite these variances, children tend to fall within one of the five general personality types.

The diagrams on pp. 114–122 illustrate the predominant personality types and general characteristics of each. Also explained is how to motivate each type of child so that he or she will want to respond in a positive manner.

When motivating a child by using his or her "natural bent" it is important to learn the child's basic interests and talents. You can use this knowledge to motivate that child to be a better student, eat healthier foods, read books, and do many other things.

Kari is a lot like the peacemaker and her strong interest is to become a school teacher. We have used this goal to motivate her to eat healthier foods, play on the high school basketball team, and study more diligently in school by showing her that she will be better prepared physically and mentally to be a good teacher.

When our ten-year-old son Michael told us he wanted to be a pro football player, we used this goal to motivate him to eat more nutritional foods and take care of his body. "Have you ever met an unhealthy football player?" I'd ask him. Now he has decided that he wants to be a zoo keeper. We have visited different zoos and talked about what it takes to be a good zoo keeper. Because a zoo must be neat and orderly, we have motivated Michael to keep his room more neatly arranged. We have given him books about animals to encourage him to be a better reader which has motivated him to do well in school. He's enjoyed doing several research papers because of his strong interest in animals.

General Characteristics	Dos and Don'ts In Motivation
• They believe they're usually right • Often critical, pointing out the mistakes of others • Perfectionist tendency • Believe there is a right and wrong way to act • Prone to "foot-in-mouth" disease • When doing a task, they want to do it right or not at all • Negative thinker • Persistent • Very loyal • Good memory of others' actions toward them • Can be warmly touched by sad stories	• Spend time fully explaining things, because once they see that certain actions are right, they usually comply • Be careful not to interpret their ability to be blunt with others as a sign that they can receive blunt, terse words in return. They are much more motivated by sincere grief, even tears, but they are experts in detecting insincere or manipulative motivation. • They like to know where they are wrong if adequate time is taken and they know if we are sincere and willing to wait until they really understand. • Avoid prolonged arguments because the "strong-willed" often feels slightly hypocritical in discussing what they "know" is right—their own opinion

General Characteristics	Dos and Don'ts In Motivation
• Conforms to others • Pliable • Dependent • Supportive • Tender-hearted • Agreeable • Avoids persistent arguments • Somewhat introverted • Careful in what they *say* or *do* so as not to cause conflict • Not the flamboyant type	• They need to know that we sincerely like them as a unique individual. • They react to being stereotyped or placed in a box. • They respond better to someone they consider a friend. • Patiently discover their personal goals and motivate them by helping them meet those goals. • If the peacemaker disagrees, encourage discussion on personal feelings and opinions rather than objective facts. • Avoid harshness or demanding attitudes because they are very stubborn when offended. • When disagreement occurs it is better to have a soft, tender conversation as you gently touch them: "You're feeling hurt, aren't you? I sure don't want you to feel badly. Let's resume this later when we can both be calmer."

General Characteristics	Dos and Don'ts In Motivation
• Manipulative • Excitable • Undisciplined • Reactive • Promotional • Expressive • Desires to be helpful • Creative • Approachable • Warm • Communicative • Competitive • Impulsive	• Discover their opinions and ideas. Help them figure out how to reach their goals in a realistic way. Many times their goals are not realistic. • "Cheerleaders" have opinions on almost everything. When motivating them, find out what they are most interested in and develop a friendship on this level of interest. • They are most responsive to a good friend who likes their ideas. • When faced with a problem, discuss possible solutions and let them come up with their *own* solutions, with your help as a parent. • If you disagree, avoid prolonged arguments because "cheerleaders" have a strong need to win. Look for alternative solutions that you both can live with. • "Cheerleaders" tend to do what you inspect, not what you expect.

General Characteristics	Dos and Don'ts In Motivation
• Somewhat like the peacemaker in temperament, but more concerned about assisting people in need rather than empathizing with them • Tends to be exacting; his way is the only way to do it. • Undependable • Impulsive • Avoids long-range planning • Conforming because they avoid conflict • Would rather do a job right than delegate it • Usually overcommitted	• They run on genuine, sincere praise. • If you expect them to do a certain job, they'll probably avoid it and do something unexpected for someone else. • They are stubborn if harsh demands are made. • They usually try to accomplish more in one day than they can finish so they become frustrated. Help them organize their day, but don't demand that they follow the plan. • If you want their help with a particular project, it is best to start it in their presence and wait for them to help. They may prefer to finish it by themselves, without your help.

General Characteristics	Dos and Don'ts In Motivation
• Objective • Uncommunicative • Cool • Independent • Competitive • Initiates action • Pushy • Tough-minded • Dominating • Harsh • Determined • Decisive	• Help them see the results of their behavior. Be objective. • They are interested in knowing what will happen, not so much why it will happen. • When an argument starts, use facts and ideas, not feeling statements. "Pushers" are motivated by cold, objective facts.

Our other son, Greg, has been taking pilot lessons since he was twelve. He is a good pilot and because of this, his sense of self-worth has increased. Because he wants to learn more about the history of flying and the various geographical areas over which he can fly, his interest in school and reading also has increased.

Greg said one of the reasons he wants to be a pilot is so that we can travel together as a team, speaking together across the country. He is planning to take public speaking classes to help him meet this goal. He also has become more interested in spiritual matters and living a consistent Christian life, because he realizes that if he is going to speak about these matters, he needs to start learning them now.

When parents use their children's interests to motivate them, the resulting progress is often amazing. Motivating a child through his interests is effective because it comes from within them. It reflects their bent.

Parents must be careful, however, not to "force" a child into a particular "bent" especially when considering the child's temperament. People can take on characteristics of other temperaments, so the five general temperaments should only be used as a guide and not a rigid mold. They can be very useful in communicating with and motivating children, but it can be very harmful to make statements like, "You're the strong-willed type, and this is the way you'll always be." Realize that they can adjust or even change their personality type in time.

2. Use the Salt Principle.

Using a child's interest can motivate very effectively, but what are we as parents to do if we can't even get their attention? What if they avoid our attempts to enter into a serious discussion with them? I have found a simple tool that can grab and keep their attention. It's called the *Salt Principle.*

We were driving back to Phoenix from Los Angeles a few years ago. Norma and the boys were in the back of our camper, and Kari was sitting up front next to me. "Kari, would you like to date during the upcoming school year?" I asked. Shyly, she answered, "Yes."

"What type of boy would you like to date?"

"Well, he needs to be nice—polite. I want him to be sensitive. He should be interested in a lot of different kinds of things, especially sports."

"Sounds like a hunk," I said. Kari smiled, blushing a little at the name I'd used. "Kari, would you like to be sure that your dream date will come true?"

She looked at me with surprise. "Sure!"

"Well, I've been reading lately about two or three things you can do that will be attractive to a boy like the one you mentioned. Let's talk about them when we get back to Phoenix, o.k.?"

"Why wait?" Kari asked. "Let's talk about it now."

We spent the rest of our drive talking about several inner attitudes that make a person an outstanding dating partner. We discussed patience in understanding men and how they are different from women. We discussed what it means to have genuine love, and how she will gravitate toward a certain type of boy because of her temperament. It was a very profitable time, and it all happened because I used the Salt Principle.

> Simply stated, the Salt Principle involves using a child's *interests* to teach specific things that a parent believes are important.

We are all familiar with the saying, "You can lead a horse to water but you can't make him drink." But that's not necessarily true. If you dump salt in the horse's oats, he will become thirsty and want to drink. The more salt you dump on his oats, the thirstier he becomes and the more he wants to drink.

When I use the Salt Principle, I'm creating curiosity. That's what I did with Kari. I knew she was highly interested in dating, and I used that interest to share some things that would help her be successful in that area. I was able to hold her interest for hours because she was motivated.

The Salt Principle motivates children to listen carefully and thereby learn some important truths about life. I used it with Kari another time when I said to her: "Do you realize that there is something that could occur in your life this next year that could cause you to doubt God? Just this one thing could cause you to become extremely self-centered and have a difficult time in your relationship with God. You'll have a hard time reading the Bible and praying and you'll find you're less interested in school. You'll also find several other negative things happening to you."

After dumping on all this salt, I asked if she would like to discuss what it is that could cause such a devastation in her life.

"Yes! What's that?" she asked with excitement. "Let's talk about it, because whatever it is, I don't want to do it." At that point, I again shared some of the dangers of premarital sex. It was another very meaningful discussion.

The Salt Principle can be used to teach children many important lessons. Here are some guidelines for using salt effectively:

1. Clearly identify what you wish to communicate.
2. Identify your listener's most important *interests.*
3. Using their areas of high interest, share just enough of your idea to stimulate curiosity to hear more.
4. Use questions to increase curiosity.
5. Communicate your important information or idea only *after* you see you have your child's full interest and attention.

Not long ago, I wanted to teach Mike an important lesson. If I had said, "Hey, how about a Bible lesson together, just the two of us?" you can imagine the response: "Yeah Dad, maybe later, o.k.?" or perhaps, "Oh no, not one of those again." We are an ordinary family and I realize that my children often are not interested in what I consider to be important for their lives. But I can salt their interest by relating to things they are interested in. Here's how I used it with Mike:

"Hey, Mike? Want me to tell you a story?" I asked.

"No, Dad. I'm playing right now. Maybe later."

"Well o.k., then I won't tell you about a crazy, wild man who lived in the mountains, and he was so strong he could break chains and no one could hold him down and he made these horrible screams so no one would get near him."

I paused and Mike immediately piped up, "That's in the Bible?"

"Yes. And you won't believe what happened to him. Maybe sometime I'll tell you the story."

"No, tell me now, please!" So I proceeded to tell Mike the story about how Jesus healed the demoniac in Gerasenes.

The Salt Principle is a highly motivating tool when used with a child's natural bent. For example, I can take Greg's interest in being a pilot and use it to motivate him in a number of areas if I combine it with the Salt Principle.

Once I was talking to a commercial pilot, and I learned that you cannot fly commercially if you take certain types of drugs. You must swear to have never taken drugs and pass a lie detector test. I knew this would impress Greg deeply, so I arranged a meeting between the pilot and Greg.

Before the meeting, I salted Greg: "You know, there's one thing you could do which would prevent you from ever being a commercial pilot." Greg naturally was curious about what that could be, but I told him I wanted him to hear it directly from a pilot. When the three of us got together, the pilot asked Greg if he had ever taken drugs.

"Why no, I've never done any of that," Greg replied.

"That's good, Greg, because I want to warn you that if you ever do, you won't become a professional pilot. You can't even experiment with drugs or you can forget about being a pilot."

Talk about motivation. What took place in that discussion was far more effective than anything I could have said. And it was the Salt Principle that motivated Greg to listen to that pilot.

I had a high school English teacher who used salt to motivate us to read books. He would read to the class from a book. Then just when he got to the most exciting part, he'd stop reading and close the book. Naturally, we'd all say, "What happened?"

"It's in the book," would be his reply.

"What page?" we'd beg.

"You'll find it."

And so we'd dash to the library to check out the book, and many times we'd read the entire book to find out what happened. Norma used that same method to motivate our children to read fifty books one summer.

Look around and see how many people use salt. Television shows you twenty or thirty second previews of upcoming programs. They show you the most exciting scenes, but don't let you know how they are resolved. They'll show a car flying over a barrier in a chase scene, but in order to find out if it lands or crashes, you have to watch the show.

Gossip is the Salt Principle used in a negative way. You can walk up to someone and say, "You'll never guess what I heard about so and so." The immediate response is

"What's that?" If you say, "Well, I promised not to say anything about it to anyone," you have just increased the salt level even more. This negative use of the Salt Principle demonstrates just how effective it really is. It can be used for manipulation, which is very negative, or it can be used in a very positive manner.

It's important to remember that the Salt Principle stems from a desire to serve a child's real or felt needs and interests. It guides that child toward fulfillment of his goals, while helping him gain important information that is vital to becoming a mature adult.

The next area is as equally effective in motivation as using a child's natural bent and using the Salt Principle. However, using it not only motivates a child, but I have never used anything more effective to communicate with children. This is the best method I've found for causing positive adjustments between parents and children.

3. Use emotional word pictures.

During most ordinary days, family members can offend each other and experience hurtful and difficult times. They often wish that another family member could understand how they are feeling. Using emotional word pictures is one of the best ways to have others enter into our feelings and it can motivate them to stop hurting us.

> An emotional word picture is associating our feelings with either a real or imaginary experience.

Using word pictures to motivate others is identifying with them emotionally. It's motivating on an emotional level.

A teenage girl once told me how she motivated her father to listen and understand her. She used an emotional word picture relating to her father's job as an auto mechanic to tell him about something that was troubling her.

"Daddy, you know how sometimes you will tune up a

car and it runs O.K., but not exactly the way it ought to? Then the owner will bring it back and say it's not running exactly right. Frustrated, you take out all your tools and check everything again and sure enough, you'll make a minor adjustment that makes the engine purr. Well, you're a super Dad and our relationship is running along fine, but there's a little part of it that's out of adjustment. I wish we could spend some time so that I could explain from my point of view what we could do together to fine-tune our relationship."

The girl's father understood immediately because he could imagine someone returning a car for an adjustment. Because he understood how his daughter felt, a positive change occurred in their relationship.

I've used word pictures in counseling to help couples open up their lines of communication. Once, the wife of an NFL player used this graphic illustration to describe how she felt about their marriage: "I feel the way you have been treating me lately is like the way a little baby rabbit would feel out in the back yard. It's cold and raining. You've come out of the house and wandered out to the trash can and stepped right on my back and broken both my hind legs. I'm terribly frightened and I'm trying to get away." Tears welled up in her husband's eyes and he said, "I had no idea you were feeling this way. I didn't know I was hurting you like that." Once a person starts to *feel* the pain another is feeling, he increases his understanding and becomes softer in his spirit.

The use of emotional word pictures is useful for children as well as adults. Children can be affected by them at almost any age, as long as they can talk. Here are two steps for successfully using emotional word pictures. First, we need to clearly identify what we are feeling—what's going wrong or how do we *feel* about what's happening around us? Second, once these feelings are identified, we must make up a story that illustrates these feelings. If one is feeling discouraged he can say, "I feel like the color blue," or "I feel like a damp, smelly dishrag," or "I'm in cold water up to my neck in a deep well." Word pictures can be created by using things that are common to our experience: animals, water, mountains, desert, furniture, the seasons.

An example from the Bible demonstrates how powerfully motivating word pictures are. In the story of David and Bathsheba, David became sexually attracted to Bathsheba, lusted after her, and eventually caused her pregnancy. Feeling guilty about his actions, David arranged for her husband, Uriah, to be brought home from the battlefield to be with his wife. David thought this would get him off the hook, but Uriah refused to return home, saying he didn't want to offend his fellow comrades. David was angered, so he arranged for Uriah to be sent to the front lines of the battlefield where he was killed.

David wasn't motivated to repent or change until the Lord sent Nathan who painted a powerful emotional word picture. Nathan related a story of two men, one very rich with many sheep, the other poor, with nothing but one lamb. The poor man raised the lamb with his children, and the animal became like a member of the family. One day a traveler came to town, but the rich man was unwilling to take one sheep from his flock to prepare for the visitor. So he took the poor man's one lamb and prepared this for his guest.

The story angered David, who said the rich man should make fourfold restitution for the poor man's lamb. David demanded that such a man deserved to die. Boldly Nathan said, "David, you are that man." The emotional word picture was so powerful that David cried out to God in grief and repented of his sin.

Jesus Christ was a master at using emotional word pictures. He used natural things and experiences to teach truth. He said things like, "The kingdom of God is like finding a valuable pearl." Or "Unless we fall to the ground like a seed and die, we will never produce the true fruit of life." "I am the Good Shepherd." "Faith is like a mustard seed." "I am the light of the world." These word pictures illustrate truths that are understandable to man because they are put in the context of human experience and emotions.

I've witnessed the power and effectiveness of emotional word pictures in my own home. It took five minutes to help my son change an irritating habit. I travel frequently throughout the country and am often gone for several days at a time. When I arrive home, the whole family usually greets me. It is an encouragement when they rush out to hug me and yell, "Welcome home, Dad!" When our son Greg was twelve, he would usually join in the welcome, but there was a time when, after the initial greeting, he would avoid me for an hour or two. I would try to touch him or ask him what he'd done while I was gone, but he'd say, "Just leave me alone. I don't want to talk."

That bothered me. He was acting like his spirit was closed toward me, but I hadn't done anything to him. I asked Norma what she thought was wrong and she explained that Greg was probably angry because I had been gone, and this was his way of punishing me.

I wanted Greg to understand how his rejection hurt me, so one evening a couple of days after I'd returned from a trip, I took him out for dinner, just the two of us. After dinner, I made up a story relating to his participation on the school basketball team.

"Greg, suppose you made first string on the basketball team and you were playing well, and suddenly you got an injury. We took you to the doctor and he said you couldn't play for two weeks so the injury would heal. So you don't play, but you show up at practices. Then after two weeks, you're ready to play again, but the rest of the players and the coach just ignore you. They act like you aren't even there. How would that make you feel?"

"Dad, that would really hurt. I wouldn't want to go through that."

"That's somewhat how Dad feels when I come home from a trip and you welcome me home, but then reject me for an hour or two. I want to get back on the family team, but I feel you are ignoring me."

"I didn't know that," he said. "That really makes sense. I won't do it anymore."

About two weeks later, I left for a trip. As I was getting into the car after saying goodbye to my family, Greg yelled, "Have a great trip, Dad. And get ready to be rejected when you get home." We all laughed, but he remembered, and never again did he reject me when I returned home.

Emotional word pictures can be used with anyone. Try using emotional word pictures with your mate or a good friend before trying it on your children. The more you practice, the better you will become, and you will see that this simple motivating force is very powerful.

In the next chapter we'll continue sharing an additional nineteen ways to motivate children.

6

Nineteen Additional
Ways to
Motivate Children

- *Help Children Choose Their Own Goals*
- *Expect Children to Do Things Right*
- *Expose Your Children to People You Admire*

Recently, I lay down next to our youngest son, Mike, just as he was falling off to sleep. Somehow we began talking about how special he is to me. I asked him the same question I've asked many times, "Why does Dad love you so much?" Unhesitantly he responded, "Because I'm a boy and have blue eyes, right?" "Yes," I answered, "but remember there's one more big reason." He thought and smiled, "I brought you back to the family, huh?" "Yes, but there's an even more important reason" I answered. He had been a major reason I changed vocations in order to spend more time with my family. Mike thought a moment more and said, "Because I'm me." "That's it!" This special time with Mike reminded me of a major problem with motivating children.

Motivating children is a powerful way to change their behavior. However, performance to gain acceptance can cause an emotional drain on children as well as on adults. Parents should be very careful not to withhold acceptance if a child does not perform to their expectations. A healthy parent-child relationship is to accept children for who they are, not what they do. Acceptance adds to their strength and desire to change.

Again, true motivation is from within a child, not from external pressure from parents.

These nineteen remaining ways to motivate are suggested not for manipulation or for performance, but so each child can attain his full potential and experience his own goals.

1. Help Children Choose Their Own Goals

The football coach at Texas A&M asked each of his players to write down a number between one and ten, with ten being the best, representing how good he wanted to be. Jeff, a walk-on, wrote down "10" because he wanted to be good enough to play pro football. The coach then asked each player to write down specific goals for the season. Jeff set goals for weight lifting, including a bench press of four hundred pounds, running the one-hundred-yard dash in eleven seconds, and so on. The coach told the players to post their goals in several places, in their lockers and at home so they would be reminded of them at all times. Every week he had them read their goals out loud to each other and evaluate their progress. Jeff said the goal-setting procedure was probably the most motivating force he had ever experienced because the goals he was striving to attain were *his*.

We practice the same type of goal-setting technique with our children, whether it involves sports, school work, or any of their other interests. We say, "From zero to ten, how good do you want to be? We're committed to help you, but we want to understand your goals first."

In the past our children did not set their goals as high as we felt they should, and this led to some conflict. However, once we understood what their goals were, we also understood why they weren't as motivated in some areas. For example, we pushed and shoved Kari for years to be above average in her piano playing. We wanted her to be good enough to play in front of a group. We finally asked her to rate how good she wanted to be from zero to ten. She picked five—average. We had picked eight for her but that was not her goal. Consequently we practically had to sit with her to get her to practice. She finally stopped practicing when she was sixteen years old because she had reached her goal.

Part of loving children is helping them reach *their goals*— not superimposing our goals upon them. If we press our goals, their motivation won't last because it will be from an external pressure rather than true motivation from within themselves.

When helping your children choose their goals, try to expose them to people who have succeeded in areas in which your children are interested. If they're interested in both animals and medicine, set up an appointment for them to spend several hours visiting and watching a veterinarian. Something might be said during the experience to help motivate them. (If they don't faint as he patches a broken leg!) The motivational force is often more powerful when it comes from someone outside the family.

2. Help Children Visualize the Positive Results of Achieving Their Own Goals and the Negative Results of Not Reaching Their Goals

It was early in the basketball season and the team was doing quite well. But they were about to face a team which had humiliated them last year by thirty points. The coach knew he had to motivate his players, so he pulled out the film of last year's game. The game looked as bad on film as it had that night. It even captured the fans' shameful expressions, disgusted with their team.

At first that may not sound like the best motivational tool, but then the coach pulled out a film of his team winning a big game. This time the fans were screaming and cheering. "Look how well you played against that other team," the coach said. "This year you can play just as well against the team that embarrassed you last year. What do you say. Let's go get 'em!"

The coach's purpose was to help his players visualize beating the opposing team. He wanted them to see and hear the fans cheering for them, to see themselves out on the court, to recall the joy of beating a tough foe and the pain they would suffer if they failed.

A very popular high school football coach in Southern California motivates his players by finding out what each boy wants out of football. One boy might want to please his father, another wants to impress his girlfriend, while a third hopes to win a football scholarship at a major university. During practice, he might take the boy who wanted to please his father off to one side and say, "You know that play you've been working on? You're not quite getting it right. Now if you use this technique, can you imagine how proud your Dad would be when you shoot through the line and make that tackle? Can't you just picture your Dad cheering, jumping up and down in the stands?"

To the player who wants a scholarship the coach might say, "College scouts will be impressed if you use this technique. They spend hours trying to teach it to their players. Can you imagine them smiling as they see you make that play? They'll put a special note in their reports about that."

We've watched our son Michael's eyes and facial expressions as he admiringly follows in his older brother's footsteps. We know he wants to be as good as Greg in everything, especially in sports. The main reason we encourage our children in sporting events is because it can help build inner character such as patience, humility, and learning to lose and win graciously.

I witnessed the force of this motivational tool while Mike was telling me how much he wanted to be a tight end on the football team, like Greg. But he was in gymnastics and several years away from being in high school. I said to him, "Mike, can you just imagine how much fun it will be to go out for a long pass in football, catch it, and do a flip completely over the defender because of your gymnastic skills? I can see it now. I'll jab the person in the stands next to me, 'Did you see my son! He jumped completely over that guy—great move!!' " Michael was laughing and I could see he was right with me; he was getting motivated.

3. Remember the Power of Praise

If, as a father, you had less than one minute each day to talk to your children, what would you tell them? Studies show that fathers, on the average, spend less than sixty seconds a day talking to their children, and most of that time is spent pointing out negative behavior.

However, the opposite of criticism is one of the most powerful motivating forces available to parents—praise. It can be used in a variety of ways. You might give your children ribbons for good behavior. You could take a picture of your child doing something that you really appreciate and put it in an album or hang it on the wall for everyone to see.

Michael was extremely dejected after his first wrestling match. He had lost and as I walked over to him, I could see tears trickling down his face. "Michael, that was great," I told him, ignoring his tears. "Your opponent has wrestled for two years and just think, the score was only two to one after two rounds. Mike, how did you keep up with such an experienced wrestler?"

Mike looked up and said, "They cheated me. They should let me wrestle someone my own age and with the same experience." He paused and then added, "But I did put him down twice. Did you see that, Dad?" His face began to shine with excitement.

A year later, Mike had decided not to go out for the wrestling team again. But the coach told him, "That's too bad, Mike. You have very good moves and great potential in wrestling." The conversation between Mike and the coach lasted no longer than one minute, but Mike's outlook on wrestling changed completely in those few seconds. That night Mike told me his coach said he was good in wrestling and asked if he could go out for the team.

As parents, we can motivate our children through praise. Instead of mentioning to them the two things they did wrong today, let's talk to them about the ten things they did right. You'll be amazed at the results.

4. Expose Children to a Variety of Activities

Some of the motivational methods that we have discussed so far come from top university students and athletes who serve as staff members at Camp Kanakuk, a nationally renowned sports camp in Branson, Missouri. A top collegiate gymnast at the camp told me that her parents exposed her to a variety of sporting activities when she was young. They introduced her to different people, including a girl who was one of the top baton twirlers in the nation. This personal contact greatly influenced her. Her parents noticed her tremendous interest, paid for her to take lessons and later she became one of the top twirlers in the nation.

The key is letting the child choose what he wants to

do. Expose children to a variety of activities, then carefully watch their response and interest. Wait until they *ask* to become involved, then support them the best you can.

5. EXPECT Children to Do Things Right

When I was a youth director for three hundred junior high students in Southern California, I *expected* those kids to show up for activities on time, to leave activities at a certain time, to produce various programs, and to do them well. I demanded the best by my attitude, and I was always fascinated by the outstanding, creative jobs the students did with any assignment I gave them.

I have learned that children can sense whether or not you expect the best from them. If they sense that they can get away with doing less than their best, often they will do just that. If they sense that you expect that they cannot do any better, they may drop to your level of expectation. I also have seen children who were highly motivated when great things were expected of them. I still hear from some of those junior high students I worked with. They tell me that they remember many of the things they were taught because they were *expected* to learn and perform at a high level.

6. Believe Your Children Can Achieve Great Things

Imagine how little you could do if you were only able to use 8 percent of your brain. What things would you have to give up with a 92 percent loss?

Most of us would give up little or nothing at all. Most humans only use about eight percent of their mental capacity. That helps me realize how much more we are capable of doing. So many of us limit ourselves because we don't believe we can accomplish great things. Doctors say that even if we lose large portions of our brain in an accident, it's amazing what we can relearn through rehabilitation— like learning to walk and talk all over again.

Many of us have watched the TV specials where three-year-old children in Japan are trained to be concert violinists. The school attributed the seemingly remarkable feat to the fact that the tots *didn't know* that they weren't supposed to be capable of such a feat.

Our mental capacity is so powerful, but unfortunately we often talk ourselves out of achieving things that are possible. And we can talk our children out of doing what they could accomplish. "Well, I wouldn't try that," we say. "You could never be like that."

Given the right opportunity and encouragement, children can accomplish incredible things. What a miracle when Kari was willing to try basketball in her junior year of high school. She had never played any competitive sports. She didn't even understand the difference between defense and offense. But she tried out for the team and made it. In her first game a teammate threw her the ball and Kari ducked thinking it was meant for someone else. Why would anyone want to throw her the ball, she thought. She was amazed at how much she learned and improved over the year. How thrilled we were when she made her first basket, and when she started for the first time. She was so motivated, she majored in basketball at her summer camp in order to be better prepared for her senior year.

If only we wouldn't limit ourselves. God has created each of us with tremendous potential no matter what level we're starting at. As parents, we must communicate to our children that if they want to give something a try, they should do it. Even strain for it. That is one reason why I ran my first marathon at the age of forty-two. I wanted to show my children that even an "old man" can do things that appear almost impossible.

7. Help Children Develop a More Positive Self-Image

A young boy who looked on the bright side of everything was given a ball and bat by his father. The father told the boy that when he got home from work, he would play a whole inning of baseball with his son. Sure enough, when the father arrived home, he took the son out in the back yard to see what he could do.

The little boy threw the ball up, swung the bat, and missed. "Strike one," the father said. The boy tossed the ball up again, swung, and missed. His father said, "Strike two." With more determination than ever, the boy threw the ball up a third time, swung a mighty swing, missed, and spun around, falling to the grass. His father said, "Strike three. You're out. What do you think?"

To this, the optimistic little boy answered, "Man, am I a good pitcher!"

A little positive thinking can go a long way in motivation. However, the lower a person's sense of self-worth, the less that person tends to accomplish both physically and mentally. A low self-image affects a child in virtually every aspect of life—dress, conversation, facial expression, future employment possibilities, even the future of his or her marriage.

In my counseling of young children, teenagers, and even adults, I have found that certain individuals seem to be programmed to fail. But I also have found there is something we can do to enhance a person's level of self-worth.

It's essential that we get our children involved in at least one activity where they can be successful. The more successful they become in various activities, the more it raises their self-worth. We should literally help them through at least one accomplishment, whether it is playing the trumpet, swimming, painting—anything. A child may say, "I can't do that." But we must find an activity that interests the child and then let the child know that we believe in him and that he is capable of accomplishing the task.

I can still recall when my high school basketball coach yelled at me one day, telling me I was too slow. It took me years to get rid of the memory of those words ringing in my ears, "Smalley, you're too slow." When I went out for track, it was difficult for me to run because I kept reminding myself I was too slow. My low self-image actually inhibited my ability to run.

8. Reward Your Children

Parents who were trying to get their daughter to stop sucking her thumb decided that they would give her a little surprise every time she went seven days without sucking her thumb. When she went thirty days without reverting to the habit, they gave her a bigger surprise. Rewards have a way of motivating and changing behavior and they can be particularly effective with young children.

Of course, we must be careful that children do not learn to expect a reward every time they accomplish something, such as routine chores around the home. Children need to learn that they are part of the family, and that everyone must work together to do things around the home without expecting any reward.

When Greg was fifteen, we discovered a very effective way to motivate him with major chores around the house. We simply placed a list of jobs to be done on the refrigerator with the wage amount written next to each job. These were jobs that were not part of our household chores, such as cleaning the garage, weeding backyard and garden, and trimming the trees.

These jobs were open to any of our kids, but Greg would rush through as many as he could. It seldom seemed to bother our other two children that Greg earned the most money. But sometimes they would write their name next to a job signifying "Hands off! It's my job."

9. Use the Ol' "You Can't Do It, Can You?" Principle

What happens when someone tells you, "You probably don't have time for this," or "You can't do that, so I'll get someone in here who can"? If you're like me, such statements bother you, so you usually jump right in and tackle whatever has to be done. I've seen the same type of motivation work with my children. I'll say, "You probably can't handle this" or "I need someone *strong* to do this. Who can I call?" The result is that the children often get right in there and do the work.

The head of my college math department called me into her office one day and suggested I reconsider my decision to minor in math. "Gary, I know you're having a difficult time in calculus," she said, "I'm not sure you can handle the more advanced courses."

I boiled inside. "Hey, wait a minute," I thought. "Are you telling me that I can't handle math? I'll show you." I politely asked for a chance to prove I could do it. She gave me that chance and, motivated to study harder, I went on to graduate with a minor in math.

While this technique can be very successful, it must be used carefully. If used on a person with a low self-image or someone who has trouble believing in himself, you may only succeed in discouraging him further, or causing him to give up completely.

10. Expose Your Children to People You Admire

My children's inner motivation has greatly increased by exposing them to some very successful people. I've taught at several pro athlete's conferences and my children have come to know Bob Breunig, the all-star linebacker for the Dallas Cowboys. Bob and Mary Breunig can talk to our daughter Kari at any time about any subject and she absorbs every word they say. The same thing occurs with Steve Largent, the all-pro receiver for the Seattle Seahawks. Our children already know of his personal faith in Jesus Christ, and when Steve takes time to sit down with our kids and chat, they remember what he says and are motivated by his encouraging words. They never forget these special encounters.

Chuck Snyder, a very successful businessman from Seattle, visits with us a few times each year. When he does, he usually takes Kari out for lunch. Each time he brings her home, it is obvious that Chuck has influenced her life. He carefully listens to her, he praises her, and he really encourages her.

Not long ago, I asked Chuck to help Kari clarify her goals in life. When she came home from their luncheon, she enthusiastically announced that she now knew exactly what her goals were. The impact was tremendous. Not only did she set her own goals, but she began helping us all with our goals. Her motivation level tripled after this one meeting with Chuck. An evening spent dining and conversing with these quality people is such an inspirational experience for my children. I'm not sure I can have the same type of *instant* impact on them. There is no amount of money I could pay Bob Breunig, Steve Largent, and Chuck Snyder or any of the other leaders for what they have taught our kids.

You may be saying, "Well, that's fine for you who know some of these pro athletes and business leaders, but what about me? I don't know people like that."

You might be amazed how easy it is to rub shoulders with some of these outstanding people. Many of them want to share their lives with others, particularly young people. There are many influential people who would love to meet with your children, if only for a few minutes, so that some of the qualities that have made them successful could rub off on your children.

For example, consider inviting your pastor to dinner. Prepare for the time by asking him to share how he started in the ministry and let the discussion after dinner stimulate and inspire your children. Try the same experience with a businessman you admire or an outstanding leader in your community. Let these leaders know what your purpose is. Invite a retired missionary or statesman to your home. Take your children to visit a prison facility. Have them ask some of the administration officials why people generally get into trouble. Try to spend time with someone of influence at least two or three times each year.

11. Be Persistent

As a parent, I never realized how motivational persistence can be. But knowing this, we must be careful to not confuse persistence with nagging. Nagging is basically negative, a criticism of someone who is not acting in the manner in which we would like him to. Nagging usually reflects selfishness: "You haven't started to clean your room yet? You didn't do it yesterday. When are you ever going to get that room cleaned up?" The same topic and the same tone of voice, repeated over and over again, can cause resistance in children and can eventually lower their self-image. They begin to believe what they continually hear—"I can't do anything right."

Persistence, however, is when we creatively and enthusiastically bring up something that we believe to be important. We mention it in different ways and at different times and in different tones of voice.

Many years ago, I came to the conclusion that everyone in our family, myself included, was watching too much television. We were hooked. I was watching too much sports, the kids were watching too many cartoon programs, Norma was hooked on "soaps." I felt uneasy about the control TV seemed to be having over our lives. Yet every time I mentioned the subject I was met with a howling reaction. I soon realized it was my fault. I was nagging with statements like, "Let's stop watching television," or,

"This TV set ought to go." These types of statements did nothing but create negative feelings and reactions to me. No one was motivated to change.

Once I realized what was happening, I decided to become persistent in a calm, loving way. I said things like, "I would really be grateful if we would cut back on the amount of time we spend in front of the TV." Then for weeks I would say no more, because I didn't want to pressure anyone. A few weeks later, I made a statement about how much TV we were watching, but again, I dropped the matter immediately.

To set an example, I began to spend less time in front of the "tube" myself. Often I'd read in another room. However, I was careful not to appear like I was superior, "Mr. Good Guy." I watched certain programs from time to time, but they were carefully selected. The most powerful statement I made, but didn't realize it until later, was after dinner one evening. I casually mentioned that it would really make me happy if someday we could live in a home where we didn't need a TV because we enjoyed life so much without it. But I added, "That's probably not possible."

About a year later, Norma called me at work and mentioned that she and the kids had a surprise for me. When I opened the front door, the kids were all giggling and Norma was smiling. I took a glance around the house, but I couldn't figure out the surprise.

"Don't you see it, Dad?" the kids yelled. "You mean you really can't see it?" I couldn't see "it." Finally, they pointed toward the table where our TV used to sit. The table was empty.

"What do you think, Dad?" they asked. I was speechless. They had put the TV in the attic. They wanted to go "cold turkey" and forget about TV, at least until they had gained control over their habit.

I was overwhelmed and immediately wanted to do something for them since they had changed their life pattern for me. I reached for my wallet and said, "Hey, let's all go out for dinner."

Their reaction astounded me again. They didn't want me to repay them. They didn't put the TV away thinking they would get some reward. They told me they did it out of appreciation for my feelings. They did it out of love. I truly felt the love in what they had done. I never sensed that they were pressured into putting the set away. After a year or so we brought the TV back, and we watch occasional programs together. But now TV doesn't control our lives. We control the TV.

12. Be Enthusiastic

Waking up in the morning has never been one of the highlights of my day. I'm one of those people who has to drag himself into the shower to wake up. Norma, on the other hand, is one of those people who wakes up every morning with a smile on her face. She starts singing as soon as her feet hit the floor. She even makes up her own songs. She is excited about seeing the new day, and her enthusiasm fills the whole house. Because of her attitude, everyone feels a lot better about getting up and going to school, to work, or doing whatever has to be done that day.

Being around an enthusiastic person is like being around someone who is laughing. It's contagious. Even when you don't know what someone is laughing about, you start grinning, then chuckling, and before long, you're laughing too.

I have found that, as a parent, if I am really excited about something, my family tends to get excited too.

One year I spent several months trying to convince my family to spend four weeks at an outstanding summer camp. But no one was even interested in hearing about it. Whenever I brought up the camp, I was met with disinterest. Later I met with a musical recording artist who had spent some time at the camp and he gave me all the enthusiasm I needed. That evening, I telephoned home and asked everyone to pick up an extension.

"Are you ready for this?" I asked enthusiastically. "Listen to this great place I just heard about." I went on to describe the camp in full. I told them in detail about all the fantastic activities available, the food, the lakes, slides, and giant water balloons. When I finished, I asked, "Have you ever heard of a place like this?" Their response was "No." They wanted to hear more. Then I told them it was the same place I had been talking about. We all signed up to go that night. Enthusiasm is contagious!

13. Develop Strong Inner Convictions

I believe it is very important that parents periodically evaluate their convictions. What do we believe is right for the family, and what do we believe is wrong? What is right for our children and what is wrong for them? What does the Bible say is proper behavior, and what is behavior that contradicts God's standards?

The average woman probably has no idea how tremendously influential and motivating she can be if she has deep convictions. The Old Testament speaks of a "virtuous" woman. It says that when you find a woman like that, you have found a woman more precious than jewels. In the Hebrew language, a "virtuous" woman was one who had strong convictions and who had influence because of her convictions.

If a woman believes it is very important for children to learn communication skills, for example, she will tend to spend time gathering information on how to teach such skills to her children. She will be *alert* to anything that will help her attain her goal. Her conviction that it's important for her children to know these skills greatly increases the likelihood that they will learn them.

This is a major reason why children learn from their parents nonverbally. When parents approve of what their children are doing, they get excited, and it shows in their eyes, their facial expressions, their nonverbal actions. Our children understand this nonverbal communication, and they tend to get excited, too. When we are displeased, we display negative facial reactions such as frowning and tightening our lip muscles.

Nonverbal communication can be a very motivating factor for children because they are alert to facial expressions and body language. The stronger our convictions, the more our nonverbal language will communicate those convictions.

How many people have had a lasting influence on your life? Think about it. They probably were people with strong convictions. The same is true for us. The stronger our convictions, the greater our influence on the people around us.

When talking with some of the Dallas Cowboys football players, I have learned that Coach Tom Landry has very strong convictions about how to play football. He has his ideas about how to prepare the offense and defense. The players say they can feel his convictions. Even the television audience can sense his seriousness as the camera scans the sidelines on Sunday afternoons.

14. Use Contracts

Chapter 5 covered how we involve our children in drawing up our contracts. We have found it very motivating for a child to conform to a contract that he has helped prepare. We have watched our children make adjustments in their lives because they have agreed to terms of the contract. For example, Greg decided on his own to change schools, with our blessing, after we had written out a contract that outlined the major reasons children attend school. After he saw the finished contract, he suggested a change. The school he was attending didn't include some of the important areas we had written into the contract. Here's a sample of that contract.

A school should include:
- activities that involve the whole family
- students that I can develop close friendships with because we have many things in common
- an atmosphere where students can pray and interact about their faith in God

There were also several other factors involved. More items were added to this list by our other children. Then together we all chose the school we felt came the closest to our contract on schooling.

15. Encouragement from Peers

When Greg started attending a new high school, he wanted to try out for the basketball team. But he held himself back because he didn't think he was good enough. During the year, he ate lunch with some of the players and shot some baskets with them after school. When the players told Greg he should try out for the team, their encouragement was just the motivation he needed. He did try out the following year and made the team.

Then there was a thirty-second, life-changing experience for Kari. Kari almost dropped out of basketball after practice one evening. I went into the gym to pick her up, and as we walked off the court she announced, "That's it, I've had it. I just can't play basketball!" The front gates were locked so we had to walk around the school and in front of the boy's locker area. When the boy's team saw Kari, they were so excited about her trying basketball that they were patting her on the back and saying things like, "Hey,

Kari, go for it!" Thirty seconds later as we were driving home she said, "Dad, I really like basketball. In fact, I can't remember now why I wanted to quit."

16. Create a Positive Successful Experience

Many times we fear that if our children get involved in a certain activity they will fail because they lack some basic skills or knowledge. We have this inner sense that tells us, "I don't think they can handle this," or, "I don't think they're ready for this."

In such cases, I believe it is appropriate for us, as parents, to intervene to help our children gain the *knowledge* or *skills* that they need before attempting an activity that appears to be certain failure.

17. Wait for the Children to Act on Their Own

From time to time, parents must "light a fire" under their children. But there are also times that we need to wait for our children to see what we see. We have found, for example, that it occasionally is very motivating to allow our children to let their rooms become extremely messy. Eventually, they get upset with the contrast between their messy rooms and the other orderly rooms in the house. Before long, they become tired of the mess and the room gets cleaned. If a child has never lived with the mess and disorder, it's harder to appreciate order.

It is true, of course, that some children will never clean their rooms without direction from a parent. But the idea is to give a child time to initiate the desired behavior himself.

18. Accountability and Support

When we share our goals with others, whether with family members or friends, we become increasingly motivated to attain these goals because we know we will be held accountable. There is a great deal of discomfort associated with knowing that we have not attained our goals, and that others we care about know this, too. This feeling of accountability, when coupled with support, is a tremendous motivating factor.

When we get discouraged or disappointed that we haven't progressed as far as we would like, the support of our family and friends can generate energy within us. This energy drives us to go forward, even when many times it seems easier to give up. Just having someone say, "How are you doing?" or "You can do it," is tremendously energizing.

19. Tender Touching and Listening

Children can become discouraged for a number of reasons—an injury, lack of progress, knowing there is always someone who is just a little bit better. Any of these reasons can make a child lose his energy. The easiest way for children to regain that energy is for someone who cares to put his arm around them, touch their hand, or pat them on the back. When someone really listens to how they are feeling, it pumps energy into them and motivates them to pick up at the point where they otherwise would have quit in discouragement.

While training for my first marathon, I was running on the shoulder of a major freeway in Portland, Oregon. Lost in my thoughts, I was startled by a motorist shouting at me with his fist clenched in what appeared to be a hostility toward runners. Then I noticed his smile and heard him shout, "Go for it! It's great to see you out here! You can do it!" Tears came to my eyes as he drove off and a burst of energy surged through my body. I literally bounced down the highway. Support like that is highly motivating.

When a child is discouraged, try the touching and listening approach: "Tell me about it," you say as you put your arm around the child. "You're really hurting today, aren't you? Do you want to talk about it?" or "I know it's hard, but you can do it."

As you touch your child, you are not only sharing with him, you are energizing him. You are not pitying him, as that can bring you both down. What you are doing is touching to listen, to understand.

After trying this, let some time go by before you start telling your child how to get back on course. Sometimes we try to get everything corrected too quickly and we drain the child's energy. Give him time. You'll be surprised at just how energizing touching and listening alone can be.

With any motivational tool, we must remember that lasting motivation must come from *within* the child. Motivational techniques such as coercion, threats, and bribing are only temporary. Our job as parents is to help our children set goals and believe in them enough to see them accomplished, and whenever possible, use our resources to help them achieve those goals.

7

The Secret
of a Close-Knit
Family

- *Six Characteristics of a Close-Knit Family*
- *Sharing Life Experiences Together*
- *Dealing with Difficulties in a Positive Manner*
- *Three Practical Ways to Share Life Together*

The muscles of my left thigh were beginning to ache. Pain shot from my knee as I pounded past the fifteen-mile marker. I had been running for two hours, and so far the enthusiasm of this being my first marathon had kept me going. But now, doubts caused by this week-old muscle pull began to creep into my mind as several runners passed me. I started to wonder if I would even make it to the finish line.

The faces of the crowd lining Scottsdale Road were a blur. I was only vaguely aware of encouraging shouts from spectators. Then the words "Way to go, Dad!" broke through the haze. My entire family—Norma, Kari, Greg, and Michael—were screaming and waving at me. As I passed them, they joined in step with me and their enthusiasm filled me with a new surge of energy. Norma and Kari ran a few steps, then said they'd meet me at the finish line, but Michael and Greg wanted to keep me company.

The pain in my leg faded as I enjoyed this special moment with my boys. I was too tired to say anything as we ran, but their company made me feel great. After three more miles, Michael, who was only nine years old, was obviously too tired to continue. I left him at a corner and told him to wait for his mother to pick him up.

Nearly two hours later, I finished the race with Greg not far behind. Exhilarated by my achievement, I claimed my T-shirt and certificate and accepted congratulations and hugs from Norma and Kari. It took me a few moments to notice that their faces were filled with concern. "I'm feeling fine," I told them, but that wasn't the problem.

Norma took me by the arm and pulled me away from our two children. "We've lost Michael," she said. "He's been lost for over two hours."

I started to think back to the thousands of people lining the streets and immediately was concerned about our little blond, blue-eyed boy. I recalled newspaper stories about a child kidnapper and molester in the area and began to wonder if Michael might have become the next victim.

We headed over to the nearest police car and filed a missing person report. As I finished the description, Greg asked if he could talk to me alone. He looked right in my eyes and said very tenderly, "Dad, if we don't find Michael, can I have his bedroom?"

Greg has always had the ability to calm us in the midst of tense situations. However, I was glad Norma didn't hear this comment, for she probably would not have taken it with such amusement. But now I was relaxed. A few minutes later, Michael found us, having walked in with some runners who were late finishing the race.

That evening, we were able to laugh together at the whole incident, and I realized that this was another example of the secret to our close-knit family. This secret is a factor common to every close-knit family that I have observed.

Dr. Nick Stinnett of the University of Nebraska supervised a study of several intimate families nationwide, families that had a great deal of happiness and parent/child satisfaction. For the purpose of the study, he focused only on families with a husband, wife, and at least one child living at home. However, the close-knit secret also applies to single-parented families or any small group for that matter.

Six Characteristics of a Close-Knit Family

Dr. Stinnett discovered that there were six consistent characteristics among these families. First, family members expressed a high degree of appreciation for each other. Several families even created projects around the house to stimulate praise. For example, one household of five had an event Dr. Stinnett called "bombardment." Every few months, the family members would meet and each would spend one minute praising every other member of the family. Sometimes the sessions were a little embarrassing, but they certainly were stimulating and inspirational.

Second, these families spent a great deal of time together. They genuinely enjoyed being together. They *worked* at doing things that involved every member of the family.

The third characteristic was that these successful families had good communication patterns. They spent time talking to each other. The key to effective communication, according to Dr. Stinnett, was that members listened and worked at understanding each other.

Fourth, the families had a strong sense of commitment. They actively promoted one another's happiness and welfare. An example of this commitment was in how these families handled themselves when things became too hectic, causing them to spend less time together. In one home, each family member made a list of his or her individual activities. The things they really didn't want to do or that weren't very important were scratched to provide more time for family involvement.

The fifth common ingredient was a high degree of religious orientation. These families participated in church activities together. They were committed to a spiritual lifestyle.

The final characteristic was that they had an ability to deal with crises in a positive manner. This isn't to say that they enjoyed crises, but even in the worst situations they were able to find some positive element, no matter how tiny, and focus on that.

For the remainder of this book, I want to focus on two of these factors, which I feel are the most important. Together they form the secret to developing intimate families:

1. Spending time together lays the foundation for close-knit families.

2. Close-knit families have the ability to deal with crises in a positive manner.

1. Sharing Life Experiences Together

Several years ago I used to speak to groups of four hundred to two thousand people in fifty cities annually. I began to notice that certain families in the audiences experienced unusually happy interaction among themselves. I was intrigued by this and began to do a study. I would interview the wife, husband, and children separately. Each person was asked the same question: What do you believe is the main reason you are all so close and happy as a family?

What I found amazed me. Each family member gave basically the same answer: "We do a lot of things together."

I found that these families also had one particular activity in common—camping. A minister in South Dakota echoed this idea. He told me that when he has asked each of his children separately what was the best thing they had done as a family, each one answered "camping." I'm not necessarily advocating camping. We've camped as a family for over fifteen years and we've found that *camping* is not the secret! But I believe the secret to being a close-knit family almost always can be found *in* camping.

One reason our family is so close is that we maximize our togetherness and minimize our times apart. That's not to say that we can't be alone as individuals. I work every day. My wife operates our office. Our children go to school. My wife enjoys swimming and going to the gym alone. I enjoy reading a book or watching a television program by myself, and I love running alone. All of us go our separate ways almost every day.

But for the most part, we try to discipline ourselves as a family to organize times when we are all together. For example, every Friday night is family night. We also share our church life together and visit friends' homes together. We share the entire summer together; my family travels with me to various seminars where I speak, and we plan a special vacation. We spend two weeks together at Christmas, another at Easter, and take weekends for various special activities throughout the year. Because of my profession, I am able to take off with the family for extended periods of time, but all-day outings provide the same opportunities for closeness. It just takes a little creativity to find fun things that the whole family will enjoy. But it is very possible!

The principle is also true for husbands and wives without their children. Close-knit marriages result from partners sharing numerous experiences. One summer, Norma asked me if I would take her through a wild animal park. I accepted the suggestion with enthusiasm and borrowed a car at the camp where I was speaking. When we arrived at the park, we were given a brochure that told about the animals and explained that if anything happened to the car, we were to honk the horn and a friendly ranger would come to the rescue.

About halfway through the park, our little convertible overheated. We pulled off the road and I honked the horn. No friendly ranger came to our rescue, but several wild burros wandered over and tried nibbling the convertible top. I honked again and in the rearview mirror I saw a herd of buffalo approach us. Within moments, we were surrounded. Norma wanted me to honk the horn again, but I was afraid for fear the animals might stampede and crush the car. One of the buffaloes bent down on my side of the car and pushed his head against the window. His nostrils were steaming the window while his big, brown eyes looked to see if we had anything to eat. Norma and I held hands, trying to comfort each other. I couldn't stand to look, but kept asking, "Is he gone yet?" "No," said Norma. "Will you please honk the horn?"

"I can't. Just listen to him breathe."

"That's not him breathing. That's me!"

Gradually, the buffalo lost interest in us and moved on. Forty-five minutes after we had pulled off the road, we were able to start the car and drive through the rest of the park. It is experiences like that which we have shared as a couple or family that provide great memories. Common experiences draw people together.

Professional athletes tell me the hardest part of retirement is that they miss the camaraderie of their team. That unique bond is built through hard training and competition together over months and years. That closeness should be a part of every family.

One summer my sons and I went fishing in Washington.

We found an incredible waterfall dropping into a beautiful pool. Having fished since I was in the third grade, I knew exactly how to catch the trout in this water. Michael and Greg weren't experienced, but they insisted on preparing their own lines. Greg did everything wrong. His leader was too long and thick. His hook was too large and his one egg didn't cover it. I had everything just right—a two pound leader, four feet long with a small hook. Although it was difficult, I left the boys and crawled around underneath the waterfall instead of staying at the front part of the pool, where there was no possibility of catching a fish.

I had cast my line and was trying to be perfectly still when I heard Greg scream. He had hooked a twenty-five to thirty inch steelhead. I, the "expert" fisherman in the family, had only caught one steelhead in my entire life. Greg, with his sloppily rigged line, had done the impossible.

I tried to scramble over to Greg to help him reel in his catch. But the rocks were too slippery, so I tried to coach him. He was screaming and reeling in his line too fast. I tried to tell him to slow down, but he was too excited to listen. When the fish reached the bank and Greg was ready to net it, the hook broke away from the line because he hadn't tied the hook properly. The fish flipped back into the water and swam away. Greg threw his pole up the hill, fell on the ground, and began to sob uncontrollably.

My heart sank for him. We both had visions of mounting this catch. In the five years since that experience Greg has never hooked another fish like it. We still look back and grieve over it, though now we can also see the humor of it.

Another incident that brought our family closer together occurred in the mountains of California's Sequoia National

Park. A small stream running over a large piece of granite about two city blocks long had created a natural, giant water slide. At the end was a dropoff into two pools of water. The boys and I immediately gave the slide a try.

After we'd each taken several turns, Greg asked if I thought he could slide down and make a little turn into a smaller pool. I looked at the slant and the angle and said, "Sure, you can do that." He took off and picked up more speed than we expected. He flew off the edge of a six-foot cliff, but from where Norma was seated, it looked like he had dropped off the mountain. He fell into a ravine, hit the granite abutment, and rolled twenty or thirty feet down into a large pool. When he hit the water, he was motionless.

Michael and I stood frozen in fear. Kari and Norma screamed that I had killed Greg. Finally I rushed down to him and heard him mumble about how his back felt broken. I was amazed he was even alive. After about twenty minutes, Greg was able to get up and walk slowly up the mountain. Within an hour, he was fine.

That experience did something to us as a family. First, *we were together.* Being together provides the basis for shared experiences that become precious memories. Second, facing difficulties draws a family much closer together. This experience particularly made us appreciate being together as we were forced to entertain the thought of life without Greg. The memories of being together on vacation when things went wrong or when we shared adventure is what *knits* the family together. As you read on, you'll see more clearly how a family becomes close-knit when it learns to deal with difficult situations.

2. Dealing with Difficulties in a Positive Manner

When we go camping, we can usually count on something going wrong: rain, mosquitoes, running out of gas, a flat tire, losing the traveler's checks, forgetting the main ingredient to a meal. When families share such conflicts, it *can* draw them closer together.

We have spent an enormous amount of time together as a family, and not all of our times are difficult. Many times everything runs smoothly. But when something does happen—something caused by an outside force beyond our control—we can recognize and accept it as a major factor that will draw us together.

Confronting such a crisis doesn't usually draw us together immediately. Frequently there is a lot of stress. We can easily become irritable and upset with each other. An important point to remember is that if conflict comes from within the family, if I get harsh and angry and yell at the kids or my wife or they yell at me, that may separate us, because it violates the principles we shared in chapter 2. A certain amount of anger or stress is natural in a conflict or mishap. But family members need to recognize this and not close each other's spirits. If the conflict has come from outside the family and we have not offended each other, we simply realize that in a few days or a few weeks we will look back on the experience and usually, in laughter, see how it has drawn us closer together.

We had an incredibly unifying experience one summer at a camp where I taught in southern Wisconsin. Kari and Greg assisted in the child-care section, teaching the younger kids of the parents who were attending the conference. After the first day, Kari told me, "I can't stand this camp. I want to stay in the cabin with you and Mom." Norma and I gave in and said she could stay with us, not realizing that it was against the rules for the children to stay in our unit.

The director of the camp section in which Kari and Greg were working learned about the problem and talked with Kari for a couple of hours. Finally, she asked Kari if she would be willing to give God a chance to change the circumstances and make the camp meaningful for her. Reluctantly, Kari agree to do so.

The very next day, the whole experience turned around for her. She met one of the sharpest fellows at camp, and they became good friends during the week. She also developed close friendships with several of the girls, and she had a great experience teaching the younger kids. She learned a valuable lesson: that God can change circumstances, even in the most difficult situations.

We still laugh about that camp experience and are amazed at the complete turnaround in Kari's attitude. She is saving her money to fly back to that camp again—the very camp she had wanted to leave.

After understanding the closeness that sharing difficulties can bring, it is almost disappointing when everything goes right. If something does go wrong, we realize it can be exciting, as well as stressful and discouraging. We know the benefit will emerge a few days or weeks later.

This second part of the secret to being close-knit is somewhat like a foxhole experience. Each man together fighting a common enemy will tend to be close the remaining years of their lives. How does this work? Pleasant or unpleasant memories lock us together. They provide common ground for conversation. Imagine being stuck on an elevator with five other people for two days. Each of you will experience common hunger, thirst, cramped conditions, fear, uncertainty, and so on. If reunion occurs several years later, all six of you will share and laugh about your unique experience, "Remember what happened the second day?" "Oh, yeah. That was terrible!" The more challenging, dangerous, and adventurous the experiences, the closer we tend to be with those with whom we share them.

It's very important to be together at various times throughout the year as families, so let's discuss some practical and meaningful ways of actually being together.

Three Practical Ways to Share Life Together

1. Schedule Regular Times Together

Because there is no way that we can effectively develop deep relationships with our children unless we spend meaningful time together, parents need to set aside a few minutes each month to schedule family time.

Spending time together is a decision that must be made and kept. There may be times when we don't want to be with the rest of the family or we feel we don't have time. That is when it is necessary to evaluate how we spend our time and what areas we can eliminate in order to schedule time with the family.

Sometimes we will plan a trip as a family and the day before one of the children will say he or she doesn't want to go. But because we already have agreed together that we will go, we do. As parents we have agreed to avoid saying, "I don't want to go," or "There are too many things to do. Let's plan this another time." Broken promises are a major factor in closing the spirits of our children. We must be careful to follow through when we plan times together.

2. Discover Each Person's Most Meaningful Activity

Once parents have agreed that it is important to spend time together as a family, they should discuss it with their children. If their spirits are closed, they may resist. But most children will say they would like to do things together as a family.

After each family member agrees to the concept of togetherness, the parents should ask each child to list the activities he would enjoy most. You might use the zero to ten scale, with ten being the most fun and fulfilling.

When we tried this in our home, Norma said her "ten" vacation would be at a place where there was shopping, sightseeing, a beach, and cute restaurants. Kari said almost the same thing. Greg wanted a place where he could fish, hike, and scuba dive. Michael's answer was almost the same, except he included playing ball. I said basically the same things as the boys.

We put our lists together and began to discuss places that were financially feasible where we could accommodate all of our "tens." We chose Catalina Island, just off the coast of Long Beach, California. The island has cute shops and places to eat. It has a beach and beautiful water. The boys and I can go hiking, snorkeling, scuba diving, and fishing. We went there for three or four days, two consecutive summers, and had a fantastic time together.

Below is a chart that might help you as a family nail down some specific activities or experiences that you could share together.

What Activities Can We Share Together in Life?
- *Our Church Life*
  study classes _____
  prayer groups _____
    when? _____
    where? _____
    how often? _____
  witnessing opportunities (mission trips) _____
    when? _____
    where? _____
    how often? _____
  helping those in our community _____
    when? _____
    where? _____
    how often? _____
- *Trips or Vacations*
  what would my dream vacation be? _____
  what would it include? _____

What are two of my favorite activities? Write an actual picture in detail of one of these activities.

What is one activity in life that I fear or feel inadequate to face? Ask family members to help me overcome this area of fear.

3. Design Togetherness Times with Each Family Member in Mind

After learning everyone's wishes for family activities and experiences, families can design a trip, vacation, or special outing that meets the needs of all family members.

Some of our family trips were disastrous because I insisted that we travel to the Colorado Mountains and camp in the wilderness next to a beautiful stream—miles from any shopping centers or restaurants. It wasn't long before we discovered that to have a meaningful family time, each person must be included—especially Mom. I could find that stream up in the mountains near a cute little village that Norma could walk to in a couple of minutes.

Our family spends one or two months every summer at a sports camp in Branson, Missouri. I'm involved in teaching and counseling while the children participate in the camp activities and are trained to be counselors in the future. There is incredible fishing and shopping nearby. It has everything we could want.

One summer, Michael and I experienced a special time at this sports camp. He had one last event in which to win a letter, archery. He was down to his last arrow and needed seven points, which meant a bull's-eye or the circle next to it. Some of his arrows had missed the entire target and landed in the woods, so he was quite discouraged. I had done well in my college archery class and was trying to encourage him and show him what to do. I felt bad for him, though, because I had this inner feeling that after all his effort, he wouldn't get the letter.

Michael pulled the arrow back, then stopped, relaxing the string. He was very nervous. I patted him on the shoulders, told him to take it easy, and said, "I know you can do it." He drew back the arrow, put it against his cheek, and let go. Bull's-eye! We both jumped up, yelled for joy, and hugged each other.

That kind of experience forms the very fiber that weaves a family into a close-knit unit. But it doesn't happen unless we recognize the value of being together and schedule times with each member's interests in mind.

Resources

Barnard, Charles P. and Ramon G. Corrales. *The Theory and Technique of Family Therapy*, Springfield, Illinois: Charles C. Thomas, 1979.

Brandt, Henry with Phil Landrum. *I Want to Enjoy My Children*, Grand Rapids, Michigan: Zondervan Publishing House, 1975.

Campbell, D. Ross. *How to Really Love Your Child*, Wheaton, Illinois: Victor Books, 1977.

Coles, Robert. "Our Self-Centered Children—Heirs of the "Me" Decade," U.S. News & World Report, Feb. 25, 1980. pp. 80f.

Drescher, John M. *Seven Things Children Need*, Scottdale, Pennsylvania: Herald Press, 1976.

Ginott, Haim. *Between Parent and Child: New Solutions to Old Problems*, New York: MacMillan Company, 1965.

Hendricks, Howard G. *Heaven Help the Home*, Wheaton, Illinois: Victor Books, 1973.

Stinnett, Nick. *In Search of Strong Families*, Lincoln, Nebraska, Department of Human Development and the Family, University of Nebraska, 1980.

Wright, Norman. *The Family That Listens,* Wheaton, Illinois: Victor Books, 1978.

Wright, Norman and Rex Johnson. *Communication: Key to Your Teens,* Irvine, California: Harvest House, 1978.

An interview with R. Armond Nicholi, Psychiatric Professor at Harvard Medical School, February 1982.